Java Threads and the Concurrency Utilities

Jeff Friesen

Apress®

Java Threads and the Concurrency Utilities

ISBN-13 (pbk): 978-1-4842-1699-6

ISBN-13 (electronic): 978-1-4842-1700-9

Managing Director: Welmoed Spahr
Lead Editor: Steve Anglin
Technical Reviewer: Sumit Pal
Editorial Board: Steve Anglin, Louise Corrigan, James T. DeWolf, Jonathan Gennick,
    Robert Hutchinson, Michelle Lowman, James Markham, Susan McDermott,
    Matthew Moodie, Jeffrey Pepper, Douglas Pundick, Ben Renow-Clarke, Gwenan Spearing
Coordinating Editor: Mark Powers
Copy Editor: Kezia Endsley
Compositor: SPi Global
Indexer: SPi Global
Artist: SPi Global

Distributed to the book trade worldwide by Springer Science+Business Media New York, 233 Spring Street, 6th Floor, New York, NY 10013. Phone 1-800-SPRINGER, fax (201) 348-4505, e-mail orders-ny@springer-sbm.com, or visit www.springeronline.com. Apress Media, LLC is a California LLC and the sole member (owner) is Springer Science + Business Media Finance Inc (SSBM Finance Inc). SSBM Finance Inc. is a Delaware corporation.

For information on translations, please e-mail rights@apress.com, or visit www.apress.com.

Apress and friends of ED books may be purchased in bulk for academic, corporate, or promotional use. eBook versions and licenses are also available for most titles. For more information, reference our Special Bulk Sales–eBook Licensing web page at www.apress.com/bulk-sales.

Any source code or other supplementary materials referenced by the author in this text is available to readers at www.apress.com/9781484216996. For detailed information about how to locate your book's source code, go to www.apress.com/source-code/. Readers can also access source code at SpringerLink in the Supplementary Material section for each chapter.

To my sister and her family.

Contents at a Glance

Contents

About the Author

Jeff Friesen is a freelance tutor and software developer with an emphasis on Java. In addition to authoring *Learn Java for Android Development* and co-authoring *Android Recipes,* Jeff has written numerous articles on Java and other technologies for JavaWorld (JavaWorld.com), informIT (InformIT.com), Java.net, and DevSource (DevSource.com). Jeff can be contacted via his web site at TutorTutor.ca.

About the Technical Reviewer

Sumit Pal has more than 22 years of experience in the Software Industry in various roles spanning companies from startups to enterprises. He is a big data, visualization and data science consultant and a software architect and big data enthusiast and builds end-to-end data-driven analytic systems.

Sumit has worked for Microsoft (SQL server development team), Oracle (OLAP development team) and Verizon (Big Data analytics team) in a career spanning 22 years.

Currently, he works for multiple clients advising them on their data architectures and big data solutions and does hands on coding with Spark, Scala, Java and Python. He has extensive experience in building scalable systems across the stack from middle tier, data tier to visualization for analytics applications, using Big Data, NoSQL DB. Sumit has deep expertise in Database Internals, Data Warehouses, Dimensional Modeling, Data Science with Java and Python and SQL.

Sumit has MS and BS in Computer Science.

Acknowledgments

I have many people to thank for assisting me in the development of this book. I especially thank Steve Anglin for asking me to write it and Mark Powers for guiding me through the writing process.

Introduction

Threads and the concurrency utilities are not sexy subjects, but they are an important part of non-trivial applications. This book introduces you to most of Java's thread features and concurrency utilities as of Java 8 update 60.

Chapter 1 introduces you to the Thread class and the Runnable interface. You learn how to create Thread and Runnable objects, get and set thread state, start a thread, interrupt a thread, join a thread to another thread, and cause a thread to sleep.

Chapter 2 focuses on synchronization. You learn about problems such as race conditions that cannot be solved without synchronization. You also learn how to create synchronized methods and blocks, and how to use a light version of synchronization that ignores mutual exclusion.

Chapter 3 explores the important topics of waiting and notification. I first review a small API in the Object class that supports these concepts, and then demonstrate this API via a producer/consumer application where one thread produces items that another thread consumes.

Chapter 4 presents three concepts that were not covered in the previous chapters. First, you learn about thread groups, which are not as useful as you might think. Then, you explore thread-local variables. Finally, you learn about the Timer Framework, which simplifies threading for timer tasks.

The previous four chapters covered low-level threading. Chapter 5 switches to a higher level by introducing the concurrency utilities, which can simplify the development of multithreaded applications and improve performance. This chapter then explores executors along with callables and futures.

Chapter 6 focuses on synchronizers (high-level synchronization constructs). You learn about countdown latches (one or more threads wait at a "gate" until another thread opens this gate, at which point these other threads can continue), cyclic barriers, exchangers, semaphores, and phasers.

Chapter 7 explores the Locking Framework, which provides interfaces and classes for locking and waiting for conditions in a manner that's distinct from an object's intrinsic lock-based synchronization and Object's wait/notification mechanism. It offers improvements such as lock polling.

Finally, Chapter 8 presents additional concurrency utilities that were not covered in Chapters 5 through 7. Specifically, it introduces you to concurrent collections, atomic variables, the Fork/Join Framework, and completion services.

Each chapter ends with assorted exercises that are designed to help you master the content. Along with long answers and true/false questions, you are often confronted with programming exercises. Appendix A provides the answers and solutions.

Appendix B provides a tutorial on threading in Swing. You learn about Swing's single-threaded programming model and various APIs for avoiding problems when additional threads are used in graphical contexts. You also explore a slide show Swing application as a fun way to end this book.

▓ **Note** I briefly use Java 8's lambda expression feature in some examples, but don't provide a tutorial on it. You'll need to look elsewhere for that knowledge.

Thanks for purchasing this book. I hope you find it helpful in understanding threads and the concurrency utilities.

— Jeff Friesen (October 2015)

▓ **Note** You can download this book's source code by pointing your web browser to www.apress.com/9781484216996 and clicking the Source Code tab followed by the Download Now link.

PART I

Thread APIs

CHAPTER 1

■ ■ ■

Threads and Runnables

Java applications execute via *threads*, which are independent paths of execution through an application's code. When multiple threads are executing, each thread's path can differ from other thread paths. For example, a thread might execute one of a switch statement's cases, and another thread might execute another of this statement's cases.

Each Java application has a *default main thread* that executes the main() method. The application can also create threads to perform time-intensive tasks in the background so that it remains responsive to its users. These threads execute code sequences encapsulated in objects that are known as *runnables*.

The Java virtual machine (JVM) gives each thread its own JVM stack to prevent threads from interfering with each other. Separate stacks let threads keep track of their next instructions to execute, which can differ from thread to thread. The stack also provides a thread with its own copy of method parameters, local variables, and return value.

Java supports threads primarily through its java.lang.Thread class and java.lang.Runnable interface. This chapter introduces you to these types.

Introducing Thread and Runnable

The Thread class provides a consistent interface to the underlying operating system's threading architecture. (The operating system is typically responsible for creating and managing threads.) A single operating system thread is associated with a Thread object.

The Runnable interface supplies the code to be executed by the thread that's associated with a Thread object. This code is located in Runnable's void run() method—a thread receives no arguments and returns no value, although it might throw an exception, which I discuss in Chapter 4.

Creating Thread and Runnable Objects

Except for the default main thread, threads are introduced to applications by creating the appropriate Thread and Runnable objects. Thread declares several constructors for initializing Thread objects. Several of these constructors require a Runnable object as an argument.

There are two ways to create a Runnable object. The first way is to create an anonymous class that implements Runnable, as follows:

```
Runnable r = new Runnable()
            {
                @Override
                public void run()
                {
                    // perform some work
                    System.out.println("Hello from thread");
                }
            };
```

Before Java 8, this was the only way to create a runnable. Java 8 introduced the lambda expression to more conveniently create a runnable:

```
Runnable r = () -> System.out.println("Hello from thread");
```

The lambda is definitely less verbose than the anonymous class. I'll use both language features throughout this and subsequent chapters.

■ **Note** A *lambda expression* (*lambda*) is an anonymous function that's passed to a constructor or method for subsequent execution. Lambdas work with *functional interfaces* (interfaces that declare single abstract methods), such as Runnable.

After creating the Runnable object, you can pass it to a Thread constructor that receives a Runnable argument. For example, Thread(Runnable runnable) initializes a new Thread object to the specified runnable. The following code fragment demonstrates this task:

```
Thread t = new Thread(r);
```

A few constructors don't take Runnable arguments. For example, Thread() doesn't initialize Thread to a Runnable argument. You must extend Thread and override its run() method (Thread implements Runnable) to supply the code to run, which the following code fragment accomplishes:

```
class MyThread extends Thread
{
    @Override
    public void run()
    {
        // perform some work
        System.out.println("Hello from thread");
    }
}
// ...
MyThread mt = new MyThread();
```

Getting and Setting Thread State

A Thread object associates state with a thread. This state consists of a name, an indication of whether the thread is alive or dead, the execution state of the thread (is it runnable?), the thread's priority, and an indication of whether the thread is daemon or nondaemon.

Getting and Setting a Thread's Name

A Thread object is assigned a name, which is useful for debugging. Unless a name is explicitly specified, a default name that starts with the Thread- prefix is chosen. You can get this name by calling Thread's String getName() method. To set the name, pass it to a suitable constructor, such as Thread(Runnable r, String name), or call Thread's void setName(String name) method. Consider the following code fragment:

```
Thread t1 = new Thread(r, "thread t1");
System.out.println(t1.getName()); // Output: thread t1
Thread t2 = new Thread(r);
t2.setName("thread t2");
System.out.println(t2.getName()); // Output: thread t2
```

■ **Note**   Thread's long getId() method returns a unique long integer-based name for a thread. This number remains unchanged during the thread's lifetime.

Getting a Thread's Alive Status

You can determine if a thread is alive or dead by calling Thread's boolean isAlive() method. This method returns true when the thread is alive; otherwise, it returns false. A thread's lifespan ranges from just before it is actually started from within the start() method (discussed later) to just after it leaves the run() method, at which point it dies. The following code fragment outputs the alive/dead status of a newly-created thread:

```
Thread t = new Thread(r);
System.out.println(t.isAlive()); // Output: false
```

Getting a Thread's Execution State

A thread has an execution state that is identified by one of the Thread.State enum's constants:

- NEW: A thread that has not yet started is in this state.

- RUNNABLE: A thread executing in the JVM is in this state.

- BLOCKED: A thread that is blocked waiting for a monitor lock is in this state. (I'll discuss monitor locks in Chapter 2.)

- WAITING: A thread that is waiting indefinitely for another thread to perform a particular action is in this state.

- TIMED_WAITING: A thread that is waiting for another thread to perform an action for up to a specified waiting time is in this state.

- TERMINATED: A thread that has exited is in this state.

Thread lets an application determine a thread's current state by providing the Thread.State getState() method, which is demonstrated here:

```
Thread t = new Thread(r);
System.out.println(t.getState()); // Output: NEW
```

Getting and Setting a Thread's Priority

When a computer has enough processors and/or processor cores, the computer's operating system assigns a separate thread to each processor or core so the threads execute simultaneously. When a computer doesn't have enough processors and/or cores, various threads must wait their turns to use the shared processors/cores.

■ **Note**   You can identify the number of processors and/or processor cores that are available to the JVM by calling the java.lang.Runtime class's int availableProcessors() method. The return value could change during JVM execution and is never smaller than 1.

The operating system uses a *scheduler* (http://en.wikipedia.org/wiki/Scheduling_(computing)) to determine when a waiting thread executes. The following list identifies three different schedulers:

- Linux 2.6 through 2.6.23 uses the *O(1) Scheduler* (http://en.wikipedia.org/wiki/O(1)_scheduler).

- Linux 2.6.23 also uses the *Completely Fair Scheduler* (http://en.wikipedia.org/wiki/Completely_Fair_Scheduler), which is the default scheduler.

- Windows NT-based operating systems (such as NT, XP, Vista, and 7) use a *multilevel feedback queue scheduler* (http://en.wikipedia.org/wiki/Multilevel_feedback_queue). This scheduler has been adjusted in Windows Vista and Windows 7 to optimize performance.

A multilevel feedback queue and many other thread schedulers take *priority* (thread relative importance) into account. They often combine *preemptive scheduling* (higher priority threads *preempt*—interrupt and run instead of—lower priority threads) with *round robin scheduling* (equal priority threads are given equal slices of time, which are known as *time slices*, and take turns executing).

■ **Note** Two terms that are commonly encountered when exploring threads are parallelism and concurrency. According to Oracle's "Multithreading Guide" (http://docs.oracle.com/cd/E19455-01/806-5257/6je9h032b/index.html), *parallelism* is "a condition that arises when at least two threads are *executing* simultaneously." In contrast, *concurrency* is "a condition that exists when at least two threads are *making progress.* [It is a] more generalized form of parallelism that can include time-slicing as a form of virtual parallelism."

Thread supports priority via its int getPriority() method, which returns the current priority, and its void setPriority(int priority) method, which sets the priority to priority. The value passed to priority ranges from Thread.MIN_PRIORITY to Thread.MAX_PRIORITY—Thread.NORMAL_PRIORITY identifies the default priority. Consider the following code fragment:

```
Thread t = new Thread(r);
System.out.println(t.getPriority());
t.setPriority(Thread.MIN_PRIORITY);
```

■ **Caution** Using setPriority() can impact an application's portability across operating systems because different schedulers can handle a priority change in different ways. For example, one operating system's scheduler might delay lower priority threads from executing until higher priority threads finish. This delaying can lead to *indefinite postponement* or *starvation* because lower priority threads "starve" while waiting indefinitely for their turn to execute, and this can seriously hurt the application's performance. Another operating system's scheduler might not indefinitely delay lower priority threads, improving application performance.

Getting and Setting a Thread's Daemon Status

Java lets you classify threads as daemon threads or nondaemon threads. A *daemon thread* is a thread that acts as a helper to a nondaemon thread and dies automatically when the application's last nondaemon thread dies so that the application can terminate.

You can determine if a thread is daemon or nondaemon by calling Thread's boolean isDaemon() method, which returns true for a daemon thread:

```
Thread t = new Thread(r);
System.out.println(t.isDaemon()); // Output: false
```

By default, the threads associated with Thread objects are nondaemon threads. To create a daemon thread, you must call Thread's void setDaemon(boolean isDaemon) method, passing true to isDaemon. This task is demonstrated here:

```
Thread t = new Thread(r);
t.setDaemon(true);
```

■ **Note**   An application will not terminate when the nondaemon default main thread terminates until all background nondaemon threads terminate. If the background threads are daemon threads, the application will terminate as soon as the default main thread terminates.

Starting a Thread

After creating a Thread or Thread subclass object, you start the thread associated with this object by calling Thread's void start() method. This method throws java.lang.IllegalThreadStateException when the thread was previously started and is running or when the thread has died:

```
Thread t = new Thread(r);
t.start();
```

Calling start() results in the runtime creating the underlying thread and scheduling it for subsequent execution in which the runnable's run() method is invoked. (start() doesn't wait for these tasks to be completed before it returns.) When execution leaves run(), the thread is destroyed and the Thread object on which start() was called is no longer viable, which is why calling start() results in IllegalThreadStateException.

I've created an application that demonstrates various fundamentals from thread and runnable creation to thread starting. Check out Listing 1-1.

Listing 1-1. Demonstrating Thread Fundamentals

```
public class ThreadDemo
{
    public static void main(String[] args)
    {
        boolean isDaemon = args.length != 0;
        Runnable r = new Runnable()
                    {
                        @Override
                        public void run()
                        {
                            Thread thd = Thread.currentThread();
                            while (true)
```

```
                      System.out.printf("%s is %salive and in %s " +
                                        "state%n",
                                        thd.getName(),
                                        thd.isAlive() ? "" : "not ",
                                        thd.getState());
                }
            };
    Thread t1 = new Thread(r, "thd1");
    if (isDaemon)
        t1.setDaemon(true);
    System.out.printf("%s is %salive and in %s state%n",
                      t1.getName(),
                      t1.isAlive() ? "" : "not ",
                      t1.getState());
    Thread t2 = new Thread(r);
    t2.setName("thd2");
    if (isDaemon)
        t2.setDaemon(true);
    System.out.printf("%s is %salive and in %s state%n",
                      t2.getName(),
                      t2.isAlive() ? "" : "not ",
                      t2.getState());
    t1.start();
    t2.start();
  }
}
```

The default main thread first initializes the isDaemon variable based on whether or not arguments were passed to this application on the command line. When at least one argument is passed, true is assigned to isDaemon. Otherwise, false is assigned.

Next, a runnable is created. The runnable first calls Thread's static Thread currentThread() method to obtain a reference to the Thread object of the currently executing thread. This reference is subsequently used to obtain information about this thread, which is output.

At this point, a Thread object is created that's initialized to the runnable and thread name thd1. If isDaemon is true, the Thread object is marked as daemon. Its name, alive/dead status, and execution state are then output.

A second Thread object is created and initialized to the runnable along with thread name thd2. Again, if isDaemon is true, the Thread object is marked as daemon. Its name, alive/dead status, and execution state are also output.

Finally, both threads are started.

Compile Listing 1-1 as follows:

```
javac ThreadDemo.java
```

Run the resulting application as follows:

```
java ThreadDemo
```

9

I observed the following prefix of the unending output during one run on the 64-bit Windows 7 operating system:

```
thd1 is not alive and in NEW state
thd2 is not alive and in NEW state
thd1 is alive and in RUNNABLE state
thd2 is alive and in RUNNABLE state
```

You'll probably observe a different output order on your operating system.

■ **Tip** To stop an unending application, press the Ctrl and C keys simultaneously on Windows or do the equivalent on a non-Windows operating system.

Now, run the resulting application as follows:

```
java ThreadDemo x
```

Unlike in the previous execution, where both threads run as nondaemon threads, the presence of a command-line argument causes both threads to run as daemon threads. As a result, these threads execute until the default main thread terminates. You should observe much briefer output.

Performing More Advanced Thread Tasks

The previous thread tasks were related to configuring a Thread object and starting the associated thread. However, the Thread class also supports more advanced tasks, which include interrupting another thread, joining one thread to another thread, and causing a thread to go to sleep.

Interrupting Threads

The Thread class provides an interruption mechanism in which one thread can interrupt another thread. When a thread is interrupted, it throws java.lang.InterruptedException. This mechanism consists of the following three methods:

- void interrupt(): Interrupt the thread identified by the Thread object on which this method is called. When a thread is blocked because of a call to one of Thread's sleep() or join() methods (discussed later in this chapter), the thread's interrupted status is cleared and InterruptedException is thrown. Otherwise, the interrupted status is set and some other action is taken depending on what the thread is doing. (See the JDK documentation for the details.)

- static boolean interrupted(): Test whether the current thread has been interrupted, returning true in this case. The interrupted status of the thread is cleared by this method.

- boolean isInterrupted(): Test whether this thread has been interrupted, returning true in this case. The interrupted status of the thread is unaffected by this method.

I've created an application that demonstrates thread interruption. Check out Listing 1-2.

Listing 1-2. Demonstrating Thread Interruption

```
public class ThreadDemo
{
   public static void main(String[] args)
   {
      Runnable r = new Runnable()
                   {
                      @Override
                      public void run()
                      {
                         String name = Thread.currentThread().getName();
                         int count = 0;
                         while (!Thread.interrupted())
                            System.out.println(name + ": " + count++);
                      }
                   };
      Thread thdA = new Thread(r);
      Thread thdB = new Thread(r);
      thdA.start();
      thdB.start();
      while (true)
      {
         double n = Math.random();
         if (n >= 0.49999999 && n <= 0.50000001)
            break;
      }
      thdA.interrupt();
      thdB.interrupt();
   }
}
```

The default main thread first creates a runnable that obtains the name of the current thread. The runnable then clears a counter variable and enters a while loop to repeatedly output the thread name and counter value and increment the counter until the thread is interrupted.

Next, the default main thread creates a pair of Thread objects whose threads execute this runnable and starts these background threads.

To give the background threads some time to output several messages before interruption, the default main thread enters a while-based *busy loop*, which is a loop of statements designed to waste some time. The loop repeatedly obtains a random value until it lies within a narrow range.

■ **Note**   A busy loop isn't a good idea because it wastes processor cycles. I'll reveal a better solution later in this chapter.

After the while loop terminates, the default main thread executes interrupt() on each background thread's Thread object. The next time each background thread executes Thread.interrupted(), this method will return true and the loop will terminate.

Compile Listing 1-2 (javac ThreadDemo.java) and run the resulting application (java ThreadDemo). You should see messages that alternate between Thread-0 and Thread-1 and that include increasing counter values, as demonstrated here:

```
Thread-1: 67
Thread-1: 68
Thread-0: 768
Thread-1: 69
Thread-0: 769
Thread-0: 770
Thread-1: 70
Thread-0: 771
Thread-0: 772
Thread-1: 71
Thread-0: 773
Thread-1: 72
Thread-0: 774
Thread-1: 73
Thread-0: 775
Thread-0: 776
Thread-0: 777
Thread-0: 778
Thread-1: 74
Thread-0: 779
Thread-1: 75
```

Joining Threads

A thread (such as the default main thread) will occasionally start another thread to perform a lengthy calculation, download a large file, or perform some other time-consuming activity. After finishing its other tasks, the thread that started the *worker thread* is ready to process the results of the worker thread and waits for the worker thread to finish and die.

The Thread class provides three join() methods that allow the invoking thread to wait for the thread on whose Thread object join() is called to die:

- void join(): Wait indefinitely for this thread to die. InterruptedException is thrown when any thread has interrupted the current thread. If this exception is thrown, the interrupted status is cleared.

- void join(long millis): Wait at most millis milliseconds for this thread to die. Pass 0 to millis to wait indefinitely— the join() method invokes join(0). java.lang. IllegalArgumentException is thrown when millis is negative. InterruptedException is thrown when any thread has interrupted the current thread. If this exception is thrown, the interrupted status is cleared.

- void join(long millis, int nanos): Wait at most millis milliseconds and nanos nanoseconds for this thread to die. IllegalArgumentException is thrown when millis is negative, nanos is negative, or nanos is greater than 999999. InterruptedException is thrown when any thread has interrupted the current thread. If this exception is thrown, the interrupted status is cleared.

To demonstrate the noargument join() method, I've created an application that calculates the math constant pi to 50,000 digits. It calculates pi via an algorithm developed in the early 1700s by English mathematician John Machin (https://en.wikipedia.org/wiki/John_Machin). This algorithm first computes pi/4 = 4*arctan(1/5)-arctan(1/239) and then multiplies the result by 4 to achieve the value of pi. Because the arc (inverse) tangent is computed using a power series of terms, a greater number of terms yields a more accurate pi (in terms of digits after the decimal point). Listing 1-3 presents the source code.

Listing 1-3. Demonstrating Thread Joining

```java
import java.math.BigDecimal;

public class ThreadDemo
{
    // constant used in pi computation

    private static final BigDecimal FOUR = BigDecimal.valueOf(4);

    // rounding mode to use during pi computation

    private static final int roundingMode = BigDecimal.ROUND_HALF_EVEN;

    private static BigDecimal result;
```

```java
public static void main(String[] args)
{
   Runnable r = () ->
                   {
                      result = computePi(50000);
                   };
   Thread t = new Thread(r);
   t.start();
   try
   {
      t.join();
   }
   catch (InterruptedException ie)
   {
      // Should never arrive here because interrupt() is never
      // called.
   }
   System.out.println(result);
}

/*
 * Compute the value of pi to the specified number of digits after the
 * decimal point. The value is computed using Machin's formula:
 *
 * pi/4 = 4*arctan(1/5)-arctan(1/239)
 *
 * and a power series expansion of arctan(x) to sufficient precision.
 */

public static BigDecimal computePi(int digits)
{
   int scale = digits + 5;
   BigDecimal arctan1_5 = arctan(5, scale);
   BigDecimal arctan1_239 = arctan(239, scale);
   BigDecimal pi = arctan1_5.multiply(FOUR).
                   subtract(arctan1_239).multiply(FOUR);
   return pi.setScale(digits, BigDecimal.ROUND_HALF_UP);
}

/*
 * Compute the value, in radians, of the arctangent of the inverse of
 * the supplied integer to the specified number of digits after the
 * decimal point. The value is computed using the power series
 * expansion for the arc tangent:
 *
 * arctan(x) = x-(x^3)/3+(x^5)/5-(x^7)/7+(x^9)/9 ...
 */
```

```java
public static BigDecimal arctan(int inverseX, int scale)
{
    BigDecimal result, numer, term;
    BigDecimal invX = BigDecimal.valueOf(inverseX);
    BigDecimal invX2 = BigDecimal.valueOf(inverseX * inverseX);
    numer = BigDecimal.ONE.divide(invX, scale, roundingMode);
    result = numer;
    int i = 1;
    do
    {
        numer = numer.divide(invX2, scale, roundingMode);
        int denom = 2 * i + 1;
        term = numer.divide(BigDecimal.valueOf(denom), scale,
                            roundingMode);
        if ((i % 2) != 0)
            result = result.subtract(term);
        else
            result = result.add(term);
        i++;
    }
    while (term.compareTo(BigDecimal.ZERO) != 0);
    return result;
}
}
```

The default main thread first creates a runnable to compute pi to 50,000 digits and assign the result to a java.math.BigDecimal object named result. It uses a lambda for brevity of code.

This thread then creates a Thread object to execute the runnable and starts a worker thread to perform the execution.

At this point, the default main thread calls join() on the Thread object to wait until the worker thread dies. When this happens, the default main thread outputs the BigDecimal object's value.

Compile Listing 1-3 (javac ThreadDemo.java) and run the resulting application (java ThreadDemo). I observe the following prefix of the output:

```
3.1415926535897932384626433832795028841971693993751058209749445923078164062
8620899862803482534211706798214808651328230664709384460955058223172535940812
8481117450284102701938521105559644622948954930381964428810975665933446128475
6648233786783165271201909145648566923460348610454326648213393607260249141237
3724587006606315588174881520920962829254091715364367892590360011330530548820
4665213841469519415116094330572703657595919530921861173819326117931051185480
7446237996274956735188575272489122793818301194912983367336244065664308602139
4946395224737190702179860943702770539217176293176752384674818467669405132000
568127
```

Sleeping

The Thread class declares a pair of static methods for causing a thread to *sleep* (temporarily cease execution):

- void sleep(long millis): Sleep for millis milliseconds. The actual number of milliseconds that the thread sleeps is subject to the precision and accuracy of system timers and schedulers. This method throws IllegalArgumentException when millis is negative and InterruptedException when any thread has interrupted the current thread. The interrupted status of the current thread is cleared when this exception is thrown.

- void sleep(long millis, int nanos): Sleep for millis milliseconds and nanos nanoseconds. The actual number of milliseconds and nanoseconds that the thread sleeps is subject to the precision and accuracy of system timers and schedulers. This method throws IllegalArgumentException when millis is negative, nanos is negative, or nanos is greater than 999999; and InterruptedException when any thread has interrupted the current thread. The interrupted status of the current thread is cleared when this exception is thrown.

The sleep() methods are preferable to using a busy loop because they don't waste processor cycles.

I've refactored Listing 1-2's application to demonstrate thread sleep. Check out Listing 1-4.

Listing 1-4. Demonstrating Thread Sleep

```
public class ThreadDemo
{
   public static void main(String[] args)
   {
      Runnable r = new Runnable()
                   {
                      @Override
                      public void run()
                      {
                         String name = Thread.currentThread().getName();
                         int count = 0;
                         while (!Thread.interrupted())
                            System.out.println(name + ": " + count++);
                      }
                   };
      Thread thdA = new Thread(r);
      Thread thdB = new Thread(r);
      thdA.start();
      thdB.start();
```

```
      try
      {
         Thread.sleep(2000);
      }
      catch (InterruptedException ie)
      {
      }
      thdA.interrupt();
      thdB.interrupt();
   }
}
```

The only difference between Listings 1-2 and 1-4 is the replacement of the busy loop with Thread.sleep(2000);, to sleep for 2 seconds.

Compile Listing 1-4 (javac ThreadDemo.java) and run the resulting application (java ThreadDemo). Because the sleep time is approximate, you should see a variation in the number of lines that are output between runs. However, this variation won't be excessive. For example, you won't see 10 lines in one run and 10 million lines in another.

EXERCISES

The following exercises are designed to test your understanding of Chapter 1's content:

1. Define thread.

2. Define runnable.

3. What do the Thread class and the Runnable interface accomplish?

4. Identify the two ways to create a Runnable object.

5. Identify the two ways to connect a runnable to a Thread object.

6. Identify the five kinds of Thread state.

7. True or false: A default thread name starts with the Thd- prefix.

8. How do you give a thread a nondefault name?

9. How do you determine if a thread is alive or dead?

10. Identify the Thread.State enum's constants.

11. How do you obtain the current thread execution state?

12. Define priority.

13. How can setPriority() impact an application's portability across operating systems?

14. Identify the range of values that you can pass to Thread's void setPriority(int priority) method.

15. True or false: A daemon thread dies automatically when the application's last nondaemon thread dies so that the application can terminate.

16. What does Thread's void start() method do when called on a Thread object whose thread is running or has died?

17. How would you stop an unending application on Windows?

18. Identify the methods that form Thread's interruption mechanism.

19. True or false: The boolean isInterrupted() method clears the interrupted status of this thread.

20. What does a thread do when it's interrupted?

21. Define a busy loop.

22. Identify Thread's methods that let a thread wait for another thread to die.

23. Identify Thread's methods that let a thread sleep.

24. Write an IntSleep application that creates a background thread to repeatedly output Hello and then sleep for 100 milliseconds. After sleeping for 2 seconds, the default main thread should interrupt the background thread, which should break out of the loop after outputting interrupted.

Summary

Java applications execute via threads, which are independent paths of execution through an application's code. Each Java application has a default main thread that executes the main() method. The application can also create threads to perform time-intensive tasks in the background so that it remains responsive to its users. These threads execute code sequences encapsulated in objects that are known as runnables.

The Thread class provides a consistent interface to the underlying operating system's threading architecture. (The operating system is typically responsible for creating and managing threads.) A single operating system thread is associated with a Thread object.

The Runnable interface supplies the code to be executed by the thread that's associated with a Thread object. This code is located in Runnable's void run() method—a thread receives no arguments and returns no value although it might throw an exception.

Except for the default main thread, threads are introduced to applications by creating the appropriate Thread and Runnable objects. Thread declares several constructors for initializing Thread objects. Several of these constructors require a Runnable object as an argument.

A Thread object associates state with a thread. This state consists of a name, an indication of whether the thread is alive or dead, the execution state of the thread (is it runnable?), the thread's priority, and an indication of whether the thread is daemon or nondaemon.

After creating a Thread or Thread subclass object, you start the thread associated with this object by calling Thread's void start() method. This method throws IllegalThreadStateException when the thread was previously started and is running or the thread has died.

Along with simple thread tasks for configuring a Thread object and starting the associated thread, the Thread class supports more advanced tasks, which include interrupting another thread, joining one thread to another thread, and causing a thread to go to sleep.

Chapter 2 presents synchronization.

CHAPTER 2

Synchronization

Developing multithreaded applications is much easier when threads don't interact, typically via shared variables. When interaction occurs, various problems can arise that make an application *thread-unsafe* (incorrect in a multithreaded context). In this chapter, you'll learn about these problems and also learn how to overcome them through the correct use of Java's synchronization-oriented language features.

The Problems with Threads

Java's support for threads facilitates the development of responsive and scalable applications. However, this support comes at the price of increased complexity. Without care, your code can become riddled with hard-to-find bugs related to race conditions, data races, and cached variables.

Race Conditions

A *race condition* occurs when the correctness of a computation depends on the relative timing or interleaving of multiple threads by the scheduler. Consider the following code fragment, which performs a computation as long as a certain precondition holds:

```
if (a == 10.0)
   b = a / 2.0;
```

There is no problem with this code fragment in a single-threaded context, and there is no problem in a multithreaded context when a and b are local variables. However, assume that a and b identify instance or class (static) field variables and that two threads simultaneously access this code.

Suppose that one thread has executed if (a == 10.0) and is about to execute b = a / 2.0 when suspended by the scheduler, which resumes another thread that changes a. Variable b will not equal 5.0 when the former thread resumes its execution. (If a and b were local variables, this race condition wouldn't occur because each thread would have its own copy of these local variables.)

The code fragment is an example of a common type of race condition that's known as *check-then-act*, in which a potentially stale observation is used to decide on what to do next. In the previous code fragment, the "check" is performed by if (a == 10.0) and the "act" is performed by b = a / 2.0;.

Another type of race condition is *read-modify-write*, in which new state is derived from previous state. The previous state is read, then modified, and finally updated to reflect the modified result via three indivisible operations. However, the combination of these operations isn't indivisible.

A common example of read-modify-write involves a variable that's incremented to generate a unique numeric identifier. For example, in the following code fragment, suppose that counter is an instance field of type int (initialized to 1) and that two threads simultaneously access this code:

```
public int getID()
{
    return counter++;
}
```

Although it might look like a single operation, expression counter++ is actually three separate operations: read counter's value, add 1 to this value, and store the updated value in counter. The read value becomes the value of the expression.

Suppose thread 1 calls getID() and reads counter's value, which happens to be 1, before it's suspended by the scheduler. Now suppose that thread 2 runs, calls getID(), reads counter's value (1), adds 1 to this value, stores the result (2) in counter, and returns 1 to the caller.

At this point, assume that thread 2 resumes, adds 1 to the previously read value (1), stores the result (2) in counter, and returns 1 to the caller. Because thread 1 undoes thread 2, we have lost an increment and a non-unique ID has been generated. This method is useless.

Data Races

A race condition is often confused with a *data race* in which two or more threads (in a single application) access the same memory location concurrently, at least one of the accesses is for writing, and these threads don't coordinate their accesses to that memory. When these conditions hold, access order is non-deterministic. Different results may be generated from run to run, depending on that order. Consider the following example:

```
private static Parser parser;

public static Parser getInstance()
{
    if (parser == null)
        parser = new Parser();
    return parser;
}
```

Assume that thread 1 invokes getInstance() first. Because it observes a null value in the parser field, thread 1 instantiates Parser and assigns its reference to parser. When thread 2 subsequently calls getInstance(), it could observe that parser contains a non-null reference and simply return parser's value. Alternatively, thread 2 could observe a null value in parser and create a new Parser object. Because there is no *happens-before ordering* (one action must precede another action) between thread 1's write of parser and thread 2's read of parser (because there is no coordinated access to parser), a data race has occurred.

Cached Variables

To boost performance, the compiler, the Java virtual machine (JVM), and the operating system can collaborate to cache a variable in a register or a processor-local cache, rather than rely on main memory. Each thread has its own copy of the variable. When one thread writes to this variable, it's writing to its copy; other threads are unlikely to see the update in their copies.

Chapter 1 presented a ThreadDemo application (see Listing 1-3) that exhibits this problem. For reference, I repeat part of the source code here:

```
private static BigDecimal result;

public static void main(String[] args)
{
    Runnable r = () ->
                 {
                     result = computePi(50000);
                 };
    Thread t = new Thread(r);
    t.start();
    try
    {
        t.join();
    }
    catch (InterruptedException ie)
    {
        // Should never arrive here because interrupt() is never
        // called.
    }
    System.out.println(result);
}
```

The class field named result demonstrates the cached variable problem. This field is accessed by a worker thread that executes result = computePi(50000); in a lambda context, and by the default main thread when it executes System.out.println(result);.

The worker thread could store computePi()'s return value in its copy of result, whereas the default main thread could print the value of its copy. The default main thread might not see the result = computePi(50000); assignment and its copy would remain at the null default. This value would output instead of result's string representation (the computed pi value).

Synchronizing Access to Critical Sections

You can use synchronization to solve the previous thread problems. *Synchronization* is a JVM feature that ensures that two or more concurrent threads don't simultaneously execute a *critical section*, which is a code section that must be accessed in a *serial* (one thread at a time) manner.

This property of synchronization is known as *mutual exclusion* because each thread is mutually excluded from executing in a critical section when another thread is inside the critical section. For this reason, the lock that the thread acquires is often referred to as a *mutex lock*.

Synchronization also exhibits the property of *visibility* in which it ensures that a thread executing in a critical section always sees the most recent changes to shared variables. It reads these variables from main memory on entry to the critical section and writes their values to main memory on exit.

Synchronization is implemented in terms of *monitors*, which are concurrency constructs for controlling access to critical sections, which must execute indivisibly. Each Java object is associated with a monitor, which a thread can *lock* or *unlock* by acquiring and releasing the monitor's *lock* (a token).

■ **Note** A thread that has acquired a lock doesn't release this lock when it calls one of Thread's sleep() methods.

Only one thread can hold a monitor's lock. Any other thread trying to lock that monitor blocks until it can obtain the lock. When a thread exits a critical section, it unlocks the monitor by releasing the lock.

Locks are designed to be reentrant to prevent deadlock (discussed later). When a thread attempts to acquire a lock that it's already holding, the request succeeds.

■ **Tip** The java.lang.Thread class declares a static boolean holdsLock(Object o) method that returns true when the calling thread holds the lock on object o. You will find this method handy in assertion statements, such as assert Thread.holdsLock(o);.

Java provides the synchronized keyword to serialize thread access to a method or a block of statements (the critical section).

Using Synchronized Methods

A *synchronized method* includes the synchronized keyword in its header. For example, you can use this keyword to synchronize the former getID() method and overcome its read-modify-write race condition as follows:

```java
public synchronized int getID()
{
   return counter++;
}
```

When synchronizing on an instance method, the lock is associated with the object on which the method is called. For example, consider the following ID class:

```java
public class ID
{
   private int counter; // initialized to 0 by default

   public synchronized int getID()
   {
      return counter++;
   }
}
```

Suppose you specify the following code sequence:

```java
ID id = new ID();
System.out.println(id.getID());
```

The lock is associated with the ID object whose reference is stored in id. If another thread called id.getID() while this method was executing, the other thread would have to wait until the executing thread released the lock.

When synchronizing on a class method, the lock is associated with the java.lang. Class object corresponding to the class whose class method is called. For example, consider the following ID class:

```java
public class ID
{
   private static int counter; // initialized to 0 by default

   public static synchronized int getID()
   {
      return counter++;
   }
}
```

Suppose you specify the following code sequence:

```
System.out.println(ID.getID());
```

The lock is associated with ID.class, the Class object associated with ID. If another thread called ID.getID() while this method was executing, the other thread would have to wait until the executing thread released the lock.

Using Synchronized Blocks

A *synchronized block* of statements is prefixed by a header that identifies the object whose lock is to be acquired. It has the following syntax:

```
synchronized(object)
{
   /* statements */
}
```

According to this syntax, *object* is an arbitrary object reference. The lock is associated with this object.

I previously excerpted a Chapter 1 application that suffers from the cached variable problem. You can solve this problem with two synchronized blocks:

```
Runnable r = () ->
              {
                  synchronized(FOUR)
                  {
                      result = computePi(50000);
                  }
              };
   // ...
synchronized(FOUR)
{
   System.out.println(result);
}
```

These two blocks identify a pair of critical sections. Each block is guarded by the same object so that only one thread can execute in one of these blocks at a time. Each thread must acquire the lock associated with the object referenced by constant FOUR before it can enter its critical section.

This code fragment brings up an important point about synchronized blocks and synchronized methods. Two or more threads that access the same code sequence *must* acquire the same lock or there will be no synchronization. This implies that the same object must be accessed. In the previous example, FOUR is specified in two places so that only one thread can be in either critical section. If I specified synchronized(FOUR) in one place and synchronized("ABC") in another, there would be no synchronization because two different locks would be involved.

Beware of Liveness Problems

The term *liveness* refers to something beneficial happening eventually. A liveness failure occurs when an application reaches a state in which it can make no further progress. In a single-threaded application, an infinite loop would be an example. Multithreaded applications face the additional liveness challenges of deadlock, livelock, and starvation:

- *Deadlock*: Thread 1 waits for a resource that thread 2 is holding exclusively and thread 2 is waiting for a resource that thread 1 is holding exclusively. Neither thread can make progress.

- *Livelock*: Thread *x* keeps retrying an operation that will always fail. It cannot make progress for this reason.

- *Starvation*: Thread *x* is continually denied (by the scheduler) access to a needed resource in order to make progress. Perhaps the scheduler executes higher-priority threads before lower-priority threads and there is always a higher-priority thread available for execution. Starvation is also commonly referred to as *indefinite postponement*.

Consider deadlock. This pathological problem occurs because of too much synchronization via the synchronized keyword. If you're not careful, you might encounter a situation where locks are acquired by multiple threads, neither thread holds its own lock but holds the lock needed by some other thread, and neither thread can enter and later exit its critical section to release its held lock because another thread holds the lock to that critical section. Listing 2-1's atypical example demonstrates this scenario.

Listing 2-1. A Pathological Case of Deadlock

```
public class DeadlockDemo
{
   private final Object lock1 = new Object();
   private final Object lock2 = new Object();

   public void instanceMethod1()
   {
      synchronized(lock1)
      {
         synchronized(lock2)
         {
            System.out.println("first thread in instanceMethod1");
            // critical section guarded first by
            // lock1 and then by lock2
         }
      }
   }
}
```

```java
public void instanceMethod2()
{
    synchronized(lock2)
    {
        synchronized(lock1)
        {
            System.out.println("second thread in instanceMethod2");
            // critical section guarded first by
            // lock2 and then by lock1
        }
    }
}

public static void main(String[] args)
{
    final DeadlockDemo dld = new DeadlockDemo();
    Runnable r1 = new Runnable()
                {
                    @Override
                    public void run()
                    {
                        while(true)
                        {
                            dld.instanceMethod1();
                            try
                            {
                                Thread.sleep(50);
                            }
                            catch (InterruptedException ie)
                            {
                            }
                        }
                    }
                };
    Thread thdA = new Thread(r1);
    Runnable r2 = new Runnable()
                {
                    @Override
                    public void run()
                    {
                        while(true)
                        {
                            dld.instanceMethod2();
                            try
                            {
                                Thread.sleep(50);
                            }
```

```
                               catch (InterruptedException ie)
                               {
                               }
                          }
                       }
                 };
      Thread thdB = new Thread(r2);
      thdA.start();
      thdB.start();
   }
}
```

Listing 2-1's thread A and thread B call `instanceMethod1()` and `instanceMethod2()`, respectively, at different times. Consider the following execution sequence:

1. Thread A calls `instanceMethod1()`, obtains the lock assigned to the `lock1`-referenced object, and enters its outer critical section (but has not yet acquired the lock assigned to the `lock2`-referenced object).

2. Thread B calls `instanceMethod2()`, obtains the lock assigned to the `lock2`-referenced object, and enters its outer critical section (but has not yet acquired the lock assigned to the `lock1`-referenced object).

3. Thread A attempts to acquire the lock associated with `lock2`. The JVM forces the thread to wait outside of the inner critical section because thread B holds that lock.

4. Thread B attempts to acquire the lock associated with `lock1`. The JVM forces the thread to wait outside of the inner critical section because thread A holds that lock.

5. Neither thread can proceed because the other thread holds the needed lock. You have a deadlock situation and the program (at least in the context of the two threads) freezes up.

Compile Listing 2-1 as follows:

```
javac DeadlockDemo.java
```

Run the resulting application as follows:

```
java DeadlockDemo
```

You should observe interleaved `first thread in instanceMethod1` and `second thread in instanceMethod2` messages on the standard output stream until the application freezes up because of deadlock.

Although the previous example clearly identifies a deadlock state, it's often not that easy to detect deadlock. For example, your code might contain the following circular relationship among various classes (in several source files):

- Class A's synchronized method calls class B's synchronized method.

- Class B's synchronized method calls class C's synchronized method.

- Class C's synchronized method calls class A's synchronized method.

If thread A calls class A's synchronized method and thread B calls class C's synchronized method, thread B will block when it attempts to call class A's synchronized method and thread A is still inside of that method. Thread A will continue to execute until it calls class C's synchronized method, and then block. Deadlock is the result.

■ **Note**   Neither the Java language nor the JVM provides a way to prevent deadlock, and so the burden falls on you. The simplest way to prevent deadlock is to avoid having either a synchronized method or a synchronized block call another synchronized method/block. Although this advice prevents deadlock from happening, it's impractical because one of your synchronized methods/blocks might need to call a synchronized method in a Java API, and the advice is overkill because the synchronized method/block being called might not call any other synchronized method/block, so deadlock would not occur.

Volatile and Final Variables

You previously learned that synchronization exhibits two properties: mutual exclusion and visibility. The synchronized keyword is associated with both properties. Java also provides a weaker form of synchronization involving visibility only, and associates only this property with the volatile keyword.

Suppose you design your own mechanism for stopping a thread (because you cannot use Thread's unsafe stop() methods for this task). Listing 2-2 presents the source code to a ThreadStopping application that shows how you might accomplish this task.

Listing 2-2. Attempting to Stop a Thread

```
public class ThreadStopping
{
    public static void main(String[] args)
    {
        class StoppableThread extends Thread
        {
            private boolean stopped; // defaults to false
```

```java
      @Override
      public void run()
      {
         while(!stopped)
            System.out.println("running");
      }

      void stopThread()
      {
         stopped = true;
      }
   }
   StoppableThread thd = new StoppableThread();
   thd.start();
   try
   {
      Thread.sleep(1000); // sleep for 1 second
   }
   catch (InterruptedException ie)
   {
   }
   thd.stopThread();
   }
}
```

Listing 2-2's main() method declares a local class named StoppableThread that subclasses Thread. After instantiating StoppableThread, the default main thread starts the thread associated with this Thread object. It then sleeps for one second and calls StoppableThread's stop() method before dying.

StoppableThread declares a stopped instance field variable that's initialized to false, a stopThread() method that sets this variable to true, and a run() method whose while loop checks stopped on each loop iteration to see if its value has changed to true.

Compile Listing 2-2 as follows:

```
javac ThreadStopping.java
```

Run the resulting application as follows:

```
java ThreadStopping
```

You should observe a sequence of running messages.

When you run this application on a single-processor/single-core machine, you'll probably observe the application stopping. You might not see this stoppage on a multiprocessor machine or a uniprocessor machine with multiple cores where each processor or core probably has its own cache with its own copy of stopped. When one thread modifies its copy of this field, the other thread's copy of stopped isn't changed.

You might decide to use the synchronized keyword to make sure that only the main memory copy of stopped is accessed. After some thought, you end up synchronizing access to a pair of critical sections in the source code that's presented in Listing 2-3.

Listing 2-3. Attempting to Stop a Thread via the synchronized Keyword

```
public class ThreadStopping
{
   public static void main(String[] args)
   {
      class StoppableThread extends Thread
      {
         private boolean stopped; // defaults to false

         @Override
         public void run()
         {
            synchronized(this)
            {
               while(!stopped)
                  System.out.println("running");
            }
         }

         synchronized void stopThread()
         {
            stopped = true;
         }
      }
      StoppableThread thd = new StoppableThread();
      thd.start();
      try
      {
         Thread.sleep(1000); // sleep for 1 second
      }
      catch (InterruptedException ie)
      {
      }
      thd.stopThread();
   }
}
```

Listing 2-3 is a bad idea for two reasons. First, although you only need to solve the visibility problem, synchronized also solves the mutual exclusion problem (which isn't an issue in this application). More importantly, you've introduced a serious problem into the application.

You've correctly synchronized access to stopped, but take a closer look at the synchronized block in the run() method. Notice the while loop. This loop is unending because the thread executing the loop has acquired the lock to the current StoppableThread object (via synchronized(this)), and any attempt by the default main thread to call stopThread() on this object will cause the default main thread to block because the default main thread needs to acquire the same lock.

You can overcome this problem by using a local variable and assigning stopped's value to this variable in a synchronized block, as follows:

```java
public void run()
{
    boolean _stopped = false;
    while (!_stopped)
    {
        synchronized(this)
        {
            _stopped = stopped;
        }
        System.out.println("running");
    }
}
```

However, this solution is messy and wasteful because there is a performance cost (which is not as great as it used to be) when attempting to acquire the lock, and this task is being done for every loop iteration. Listing 2-4 reveals a more efficient and cleaner approach.

Listing 2-4. Attempting to Stop a Thread via the volatile Keyword

```java
public class ThreadStopping
{
    public static void main(String[] args)
    {
        class StoppableThread extends Thread
        {
            private volatile boolean stopped; // defaults to false

            @Override
            public void run()
            {
                while(!stopped)
                    System.out.println("running");
            }

            void stopThread()
            {
                stopped = true;
            }
        }
```

```
      StoppableThread thd = new StoppableThread();
      thd.start();
      try
      {
         Thread.sleep(1000); // sleep for 1 second
      }
      catch (InterruptedException ie)
      {
      }
      thd.stopThread();
   }
}
```

Because stopped has been marked volatile, each thread will access the main memory copy of this variable and not access a cached copy. The application will stop, even on a multiprocessor-based or a multicore-based machine.

■ **Caution**   Use volatile only where visibility is an issue. Also, you can only use this reserved word in the context of field declarations (you'll receive an error if you try to make a local variable volatile). Finally, you can declare double and long fields volatile, but should avoid doing so on 32-bit JVMs because it takes two operations to access a double or long variable's value, and mutual exclusion (via synchronized) is required to access their values safely.

When a field variable is declared volatile, it cannot also be declared final. However, this isn't a problem because Java also lets you safely access a final field without the need for synchronization. To overcome the cached variable problem in DeadlockDemo, I marked both lock1 and lock2 final, although I could have marked them volatile.

You will often use final to help ensure thread safety in the context of an *immutable* (unchangeable) class. Consider Listing 2-5.

Listing 2-5. Creating an Immutable and Thread-Safe Class with Help from final

```
import java.util.Set;
import java.util.TreeSet;

public final class Planets
{
   private final Set<String> planets = new TreeSet<>();

   public Planets()
   {
      planets.add("Mercury");
      planets.add("Venus");
```

```
        planets.add("Earth");
        planets.add("Mars");
        planets.add("Jupiter");
        planets.add("Saturn");
        planets.add("Uranus");
        planets.add("Neptune");
    }

    public boolean isPlanet(String planetName)
    {
        return planets.contains(planetName);
    }
}
```

Listing 2-5 presents an immutable Planets class whose objects store sets of planet names. Although the set is mutable, the design of this class prevents the set from being modified after the constructor exits. By declaring planets final, the reference stored in this field cannot be modified. Furthermore, this reference will not be cached so the cached variable problem goes away.

Java provides a special thread-safety guarantee concerning immutable objects. These objects can be safely accessed from multiple threads, even when synchronization isn't used to *publish* (expose) their references provided that the following rules are observed:

- Immutable objects must not allow state to be modified.

- All fields must be declared final.

- Objects must be properly constructed so that "this" references don't escape from constructors.

The last point is probably confusing, so here is a simple example where this explicitly escapes from the constructor:

```
public class ThisEscapeDemo
{
    private static ThisEscapeDemo lastCreatedInstance;

    public ThisEscapeDemo()
    {
        lastCreatedInstance = this;
    }
}
```

Check out "Java theory and practice: Safe construction techniques" at www.ibm.com/developerworks/library/j-jtp0618/ to learn more about this common threading hazard.

EXERCISES

The following exercises are designed to test your understanding of Chapter 2's content:

1. Identify the three problems with threads.

2. True or false: When the correctness of a computation depends on the relative timing or interleaving of multiple threads by the scheduler, you have a data race.

3. Define synchronization.

4. Identify the two properties of synchronization.

5. How is synchronization implemented?

6. True or false: A thread that has acquired a lock doesn't release this lock when it calls one of Thread's sleep() methods.

7. How do you specify a synchronized method?

8. How do you specify a synchronized block?

9. Define liveness.

10. Identify the three liveness challenges.

11. How does the volatile keyword differ from synchronized?

12. True or false: Java also lets you safely access a final field without the need for synchronization.

13. Identify the thread problems with the following CheckingAccount class:

```
public class CheckingAccount
{
    private int balance;
    public CheckingAccount(int initialBalance)
    {
        balance = initialBalance;
    }
    public boolean withdraw(int amount)
    {
        if (amount <= balance)
        {
            try
```

```
                {
                    Thread.sleep((int) (Math.random() * 200));
                }
                catch (InterruptedException ie)
                {
                }
                balance -= amount;
                return true;
            }
            return false;
        }
        public static void main(String[] args)
        {
            final CheckingAccount ca = new CheckingAccount(100);
            Runnable r = new Runnable()
                        {
                            @Override
                            public void run()
                            {
                                String name = Thread.currentThread().
                                getName();
                                for (int i = 0; i < 10; i++)
                                    System.out.println (name + "
                                    withdraws $10: " +
                                                    ca.withdraw(10));
                            }
                        };
            Thread thdHusband = new Thread(r);
            thdHusband.setName("Husband");
            Thread thdWife = new Thread(r);
            thdWife.setName("Wife");
            thdHusband.start();
            thdWife.start();
        }
    }
```

14.   Fix the thread problems in the previous CheckingAccount class.

Summary

Developing multithreaded applications is much easier when threads don't interact,
typically via shared variables. When interaction occurs, race conditions, data races, and
cached variable problems can arise that make an application thread-unsafe.

You can use synchronization to solve race conditions, data races, and cached
variable problems. Synchronization is a JVM feature that ensures that two or more
concurrent threads don't simultaneously execute a critical section that must be accessed
in a serial manner.

Liveness refers to something beneficial happening eventually. A liveness failure occurs when an application reaches a state in which it can make no further progress. Multithreaded applications face the liveness challenges of deadlock, livelock, and starvation.

Synchronization exhibits two properties: mutual exclusion and visibility. The synchronized keyword is associated with both properties. Java also provides a weaker form of synchronization involving visibility only, and associates only this property with the volatile keyword.

When a field variable is declared volatile, it cannot also be declared final. However, this isn't a problem because Java also lets you safely access a final field without the need for synchronization. You will often use final to help ensure thread safety in the context of an immutable class.

Chapter 3 presents waiting and notification.

CHAPTER 3

■ ■ ■

Waiting and Notification

Java provides a small API that supports communication between threads. Using this API, one thread waits for a *condition* (a prerequisite for continued execution) to exist. In the future, another thread will create the condition and then notify the waiting thread. In this chapter, I introduce you to this API.

Wait-and-Notify API Tour

The java.lang.Object class provides a Wait-and-Notify API that consists of three wait() methods, one notify() method, and one notifyAll() method. The wait() methods wait for a condition to exist; the notify() and notifyAll() methods notify waiting threads when the condition exists:

- void wait(): Cause the current thread to wait until another thread invokes the notify() or notifyAll() method for this object, or for some other thread to interrupt the current thread while waiting.

- void wait(long timeout): Cause the current thread to wait until another thread invokes the notify() or notifyAll() method for this object, or for the specified amount of time measured in milliseconds (identified by timeout) to pass, or for some other thread to interrupt the current thread while waiting. This method throws java.lang.IllegalArgumentException when timeout is negative.

- void wait(long timeout, int nanos): Cause the current thread to wait until another thread invokes the notify() or notifyAll() method for this object, or for the specified amount of time measured in milliseconds (identified by timeout) plus nanoseconds (identified by nanos) to pass, or for some other thread to interrupt the current thread while waiting. This method throws IllegalArgumentException when timeout is negative, nanos is negative, or nanos is greater than 999999.

- `void notify()`: Wake up a single thread that's waiting on this object's monitor. If any threads are waiting on this object, one of them is chosen to be awakened. The choice is arbitrary and occurs at the discretion of the implementation. The awakened thread will not be able to proceed until the current thread relinquishes the lock on this object. The awakened thread will compete in the usual manner with any other threads that might be actively competing to synchronize on this object; for example, the awakened thread enjoys no reliable privilege or disadvantage in being the next thread to lock this object.

- `void notifyAll()`: Wake up all threads that are waiting on this object's monitor. The awakened threads will not be able to proceed until the current thread relinquishes the lock on this object. The awakened threads will compete in the usual manner with any other threads that might be actively competing to synchronize on this object; for example, the awakened threads enjoy no reliable privilege or disadvantage in being the next thread to lock this object.

The three `wait()` methods throw `java.lang.InterruptedException` when any thread interrupted the current thread before or while the current thread was waiting for a notification. The interrupted status of the current thread is cleared when this exception is thrown.

■ **Note** A thread releases ownership of the monitor associated with the object whose `wait()` method is called.

This API leverages an object's *condition queue*, which is a data structure that stores threads waiting for a condition to exist. The waiting threads are known as the *wait set*. Because the condition queue is tightly bound to an object's lock, all five methods must be called from within a synchronized context (the current thread must be the owner of the object's monitor); otherwise, `java.lang.IllegalMonitorStateException` is thrown.

The following code/pseudocode fragment demonstrates the noargument `wait()` method:

```
synchronized(obj)
{
   while (<condition does not hold>)
      obj.wait();

   // Perform an action that's appropriate to condition.
}
```

The wait() method is called from within a synchronized block that synchronizes on the same object as the object on which wait() is called (obj). Because of the possibility of *spurious wakeups* (a thread wakes up without being notified, interrupted, or timing out), wait() is called from within a while loop that tests for the condition holding and reexecutes wait() when the condition still doesn't hold. After the while loop exits, the condition exists and an action appropriate to the condition can be performed.

■ **Caution**   Never call a wait() method outside of a loop. The loop tests the condition before and after the wait() call. Testing the condition before calling wait() ensures *liveness*. If this test was not present, and if the condition held and notify() had been called prior to wait() being called, it's unlikely that the waiting thread would ever wake up. Retesting the condition after calling wait() ensures *safety*. If retesting didn't occur, and if the condition didn't hold after the thread had awakened from the wait() call (perhaps another thread called notify() accidentally when the condition didn't hold), the thread would proceed to destroy the lock's protected invariants.

The following code fragment demonstrates the notify() method, which notifies the waiting thread in the previous example:

```
synchronized(obj)
{
    // Set the condition.

    obj.notify();
}
```

Notice that notify() is called from a critical section guarded by the same object (obj) as the critical section for the wait() method. Also, notify() is called using the same obj reference. Follow this pattern and you shouldn't get into trouble.

■ **Note**   There has been much discussion about which notification method is better: notify() or notifyAll(). For example, check out "Difference between notify() and notifyAll()" (http://stackoverflow.com/questions/14924610/difference-between-notify-and-notifyall). If you're wondering which method to use, I would use notify() in an application where there are only two threads, and where either thread occasionally waits and needs to be notified by the other thread. Otherwise, I would use notifyAll().

Producers and Consumers

A classic example of thread communication involving conditions is the relationship between a producer thread and a consumer thread. The producer thread produces data items to be consumed by the consumer thread. Each produced data item is stored in a shared variable.

Imagine that the threads are running at different speeds. The producer might produce a new data item and record it in the shared variable before the consumer retrieves the previous data item for processing. Also, the consumer might retrieve the contents of the shared variable before a new data item is produced.

To overcome those problems, the producer thread must wait until it's notified that the previously produced data item has been consumed, and the consumer thread must wait until it's notified that a new data item has been produced. Listing 3-1 shows you how to accomplish this task via wait() and notify().

Listing 3-1. The Producer-Consumer Relationship Version 1

```
public class PC
{
   public static void main(String[] args)
   {
      Shared s = new Shared();
      new Producer(s).start();
      new Consumer(s).start();
   }
}

class Shared
{
   private char c;
   private volatile boolean writeable = true;

   synchronized void setSharedChar(char c)
   {
      while (!writeable)
         try
         {
            wait();
         }
         catch (InterruptedException ie)
         {
         }
      this.c = c;
      writeable = false;
      notify();
   }
```

```java
   synchronized char getSharedChar()
   {
      while (writeable)
         try
         {
            wait();
         }
         catch (InterruptedException ie)
         {
         }
      writeable = true;
      notify();
      return c;
   }
}

class Producer extends Thread
{
   private final Shared s;

   Producer(Shared s)
   {
      this.s = s;
   }

   @Override
   public void run()
   {
      for (char ch = 'A'; ch <= 'Z'; ch++)
      {
         s.setSharedChar(ch);
         System.out.println(ch + " produced by producer.");
      }
   }
}
class Consumer extends Thread
{
   private final Shared s;

   Consumer(Shared s)
   {
      this.s = s;
   }
```

```
@Override
public void run()
{
    char ch;
    do
    {
        ch = s.getSharedChar();
        System.out.println(ch + " consumed by consumer.");
    }
    while (ch != 'Z');
}
}
```

This application creates a Shared object and two threads that get a copy of the object's reference. The producer calls the object's setSharedChar() method to save each of 26 uppercase letters; the consumer calls the object's getSharedChar() method to acquire each letter.

The writeable instance field tracks two conditions: the producer waiting on the consumer to consume a data item and the consumer waiting on the producer to produce a new data item. It helps coordinate execution of the producer and consumer. The following scenario, where the consumer executes first, illustrates this coordination:

1. The consumer executes s.getSharedChar() to retrieve a letter.

2. Inside of that synchronized method, the consumer calls wait() because writeable contains true. The consumer now waits until it receives notification from the producer.

3. The producer eventually executes s.setSharedChar(ch);.

4. When the producer enters that synchronized method (which is possible because the consumer released the lock inside of the wait() method prior to waiting), the producer discovers writeable's value to be true and doesn't call wait().

5. The producer saves the character, sets writeable to false (which will cause the producer to wait on the next setSharedChar() call when the consumer has not consumed the character by that time), and calls notify() to awaken the consumer (assuming the consumer is waiting).

6. The producer exits setSharedChar(char c).

7. The consumer wakes up (and reacquires the lock), sets writeable to true (which will cause the consumer to wait on the next getSharedChar() call when the producer has not produced a character by that time), notifies the producer to awaken that thread (assuming the producer is waiting), and returns the shared character.

Compile Listing 3-1 as follows:

```
javac PC.java
```

Run the resulting application as follows:

```
java PC
```

You should observe output such as the following excerpt during one run:

```
W produced by producer.
W consumed by consumer.
X produced by producer.
X consumed by consumer.
Y produced by producer.
Y consumed by consumer.
Z produced by producer.
Z consumed by consumer.
```

Although the synchronization works correctly, you might observe multiple producing messages before multiple consuming messages:

```
A produced by producer.
B produced by producer.
A consumed by consumer.
B consumed by consumer.
```

Also, you might observe a consuming message before a producing message:

```
V consumed by consumer.
V produced by producer.
```

Either strange output order doesn't mean that the producer and consumer threads aren't synchronized. Instead, it's the result of the call to setSharedChar() followed by its companion System.out.println() method call not being synchronized, and by the call to getSharedChar() followed by its companion System.out.println() method call not being synchronized. The output order can be corrected by wrapping each of these method call pairs in a synchronized block that synchronizes on the Shared object referenced by s. Listing 3-2 presents this enhancement.

Listing 3-2. The Producer-Consumer Relationship Version 2

```java
public class PC
{
   public static void main(String[] args)
   {
      Shared s = new Shared();
      new Producer(s).start();
      new Consumer(s).start();
   }
}

class Shared
{
   private char c;
   private volatile boolean writeable = true;

   synchronized void setSharedChar(char c)
   {
      while (!writeable)
         try
         {
            wait();
         }
         catch (InterruptedException ie)
         {
         }
      this.c = c;
      writeable = false;
      notify();
   }

   synchronized char getSharedChar()
   {
      while (writeable)
         try
         {
            wait();
         }
         catch (InterruptedException ie)
         {
         }
      writeable = true;
      notify();
      return c;
   }
}
```

```
class Producer extends Thread
{
   private final Shared s;

   Producer(Shared s)
   {
      this.s = s;
   }

   @Override
   public void run()
   {
      for (char ch = 'A'; ch <= 'Z'; ch++)
      {
         synchronized(s)
         {
            s.setSharedChar(ch);
            System.out.println(ch + " produced by producer.");
         }
      }
   }
}
class Consumer extends Thread
{
   private final Shared s;

   Consumer(Shared s)
   {
      this.s = s;
   }

   @Override
   public void run()
   {
      char ch;
      do
      {
         synchronized(s)
         {
            ch = s.getSharedChar();
            System.out.println(ch + " consumed by consumer.");
         }
      }
      while (ch != 'Z');
   }
}
```

Compile Listing 3-2 (javac PC.java) and run this application (java PC). Its output should always appear in the same alternating order as shown next (only the first few lines are shown for brevity):

```
A produced by producer.
A consumed by consumer.
B produced by producer.
B consumed by consumer.
C produced by producer.
C consumed by consumer.
D produced by producer.
D consumed by consumer.
```

EXERCISES

The following exercises are designed to test your understanding of Chapter 3's content:

1. Define condition.

2. Describe the API that supports conditions.

3. True or false: The wait() methods are interruptible.

4. What method would you call to wake up all threads that are waiting on an object's monitor?

5. True or false: A thread that has acquired a lock doesn't release this lock when it calls one of Object's wait() methods.

6. Define condition queue.

7. What happens when you call any of the API's methods outside of a synchronized context?

8. Define spurious wakeup.

9. Why should you call a wait() method in a loop context?

10. Create an Await application that demonstrates a higher-level concurrency construct known as a *gate*. This construct permits multiple threads to arrive at a synchronization point (the *gate*) and wait until the gate is unlocked by another thread so that they can all proceed.

The main() method first creates a runnable for the threads that will wait at the gate. The runnable prints a message stating that the thread is waiting, increments a counter, sleeps for 2 seconds, and waits (make sure to account for spurious wakeups). Upon wakeup, the thread outputs a message stating that the thread is terminating. main() then creates three Thread objects and starts three threads to execute the runnable. Next, main() creates another runnable that repeatedly sleeps for 200 milliseconds until the counter equals 3, at which point it notifies all waiting threads. Finally, main() creates a Thread object for the second runnable and starts the thread.

Summary

Java provides an API that supports communication between threads. This API consists of Object's three wait() methods, one notify() method, and one notifyAll() method. The wait() methods wait for a condition to exist; notify() and notifyAll() notify waiting threads when the condition exists.

The wait(), notify(), and notifyAll() methods are called from within a synchronized block that synchronizes on the same object as the object on which they are called. Because of spurious wakeups, wait() is called from a while loop that reexecutes wait() while the condition doesn't hold.

A classic example of thread communication involving conditions is the relationship between a producer thread and a consumer thread. The producer thread produces data items to be consumed by the consumer thread. Each produced data item is stored in a shared variable.

To overcome problems such as consuming a data item that hasn't been produced, the producer thread must wait until it's notified that the previously produced data item has been consumed, and the consumer thread must wait until it's notified that a new data item has been produced.

Chapter 4 presents additional thread capabilities.

CHAPTER 4

■ ■ ■

Additional Thread Capabilities

Chapters 1 through 3 introduced you to the java.lang.Thread class and java.lang. Runnable interface, to synchronization, and to waiting and notification. In this chapter, I complete my coverage of thread basics by introducing you to thread groups and thread-local variables. Also, I present the Timer Framework, which leverages Thread behind the scenes to simplify timer-oriented tasks.

Thread Groups

While exploring the Thread class, you've probably encountered references to the java.lang.ThreadGroup class in constructors such as Thread(ThreadGroup group, Runnable target), and in methods such as static int activeCount() and static int enumerate(Thread[] tarray).

The JDK documentation for ThreadGroup states that a *thread group* "represents a set of threads. In addition, a thread group can also include other thread groups. The thread groups form a tree in which every thread group except the initial thread group has a parent."

Using a ThreadGroup object, you can perform an operation on all contained Thread objects. For example, assuming a thread group referenced by variable tg, tg.suspend(); suspends all of the threads in the thread group. Thread groups simplify the management of many threads.

Although ThreadGroup appears to be a very useful, you should largely avoid this class for the following reasons:

- The most useful ThreadGroup methods are void suspend(), void resume(), and void stop(). These methods have been deprecated because, like their Thread counterparts (to which these methods delegate for each thread in the thread group), they are prone to deadlock and other problems.

- ThreadGroup isn't thread-safe. For example, to obtain a count of the active threads in a thread group, you would call ThreadGroup's int activeCount() method. You would then use this value to size the array that you pass to one of ThreadGroup's enumerate() methods. However, there is no guarantee that the count will remain accurate because, between the time you've created the array and the time you pass it to enumerate(), this count could change because of thread creation and termination. If the array is too small, enumerate() silently ignores extra threads. The same can be said of Thread's activeCount() and enumerate() methods, which delegate to the ThreadGroup methods for the current thread. This problem is an example of the "time of check to time of use" (https://en.wikipedia.org/wiki/Time_of_ check_to_time_of_use) class of software bug. (This bug also rears its ugly head in scenarios where you need to check for file existence before performing an operation on the file. Between the file check and the operation, the file might be deleted or created.)

However, you should still know about ThreadGroup because of its contribution in handling exceptions that are thrown while a thread is executing. Listing 4-1 sets the stage for learning about exception handling by presenting a run() method that attempts to divide an integer by 0, which results in a thrown java.lang.ArithmeticException object.

Listing 4-1. Throwing an Exception from the run() Method

```java
public class ExceptionThread
{
   public static void main(String[] args)
   {
      Runnable r = new Runnable()
                 {
                     @Override
                     public void run()
                     {
                         int x = 1 / 0; // Line 10
                     }
                 };
      Thread thd = new Thread(r);
      thd.start();
   }
}
```

The default main thread creates a runnable that deliberately throws an ArithmeticException object by attempting to divide an integer by integer 0.

Compile Listing 4-1 as follows:

```
javac ExceptionThread.java
```

Run the resulting application as follows:

```
java ExceptionThread
```

You'll see an exception trace that identifies the thrown instance of the ArithmeticException class:

```
Exception in thread "Thread-0" java.lang.ArithmeticException: / by zero
        at ExceptionThread$1.run(ExceptionThread.java:10)
        at java.lang.Thread.run(Thread.java:745)
```

When an exception is thrown out of the run() method, the thread terminates and the following activities take place:

- The Java virtual machine (JVM) looks for an instance of Thread. UncaughtExceptionHandler installed via Thread's void setUncau ghtExceptionHandler(Thread.UncaughtExceptionHandler eh) method. When this handler is found, it passes execution to the instance's void uncaughtException(Thread t, Throwable e) method, where t identifies the Thread object of the thread that threw the exception, and e identifies the thrown exception or error—perhaps a java.lang.OutOfMemoryError object was thrown. If uncaughtException() throws an exception/error, the exception/error is ignored by the JVM.

- Assuming that setUncaughtExceptionHandler() was not called to install a handler, the JVM passes control to the associated ThreadGroup object's uncaughtException(Thread t, Throwable e) method. Assuming that ThreadGroup was not extended and that its uncaughtException() method was not overridden to handle the exception, uncaughtException() passes control to the parent ThreadGroup object's uncaughtException() method when a parent ThreadGroup is present. Otherwise, it checks to see if a default uncaught exception handler has been installed (via Thread's static void setDefaultUncaught ExceptionHandler(Thread.UncaughtExceptionHandler handler) method). If a default uncaught exception handler has been installed, its uncaughtException() method is called with the same two arguments. Otherwise, uncaughtException() checks its Throwable argument to determine if it's an instance of java.lang.ThreadDeath. If so, nothing special is done. Otherwise, as Listing 4-1's exception message shows, a message containing the thread's name, as returned from the thread's getName() method, and a stack backtrace, using the Throwable argument's printStackTrace() method, is printed to the standard error stream.

Listing 4-2 demonstrates Thread's setUncaughtExceptionHandler() and setDefaultUncaughtExceptionHandler() methods.

Listing 4-2. Demonstrating Uncaught Exception Handlers

```
public class ExceptionThread
{
   public static void main(String[] args)
   {
     Runnable r = new Runnable()
                  {
                     @Override
                     public void run()
                     {
                        int x = 1 / 0;
                     }
                  };
     Thread thd = new Thread(r);
     Thread.UncaughtExceptionHandler uceh;
     uceh = new Thread.UncaughtExceptionHandler()
            {
               @Override
               public void uncaughtException(Thread t, Throwable e)
               {
                  System.out.println("Caught throwable " + e +
                                       " for thread " + t);
               }
            };
     thd.setUncaughtExceptionHandler(uceh);
     uceh = new Thread.UncaughtExceptionHandler()
            {
               @Override
               public void uncaughtException(Thread t, Throwable e)
               {
                  System.out.println("Default uncaught exception handler");
                  System.out.println("Caught throwable " + e +
                                       " for thread " + t);
               }
            };
     thd.setDefaultUncaughtExceptionHandler(uceh);
     thd.start();
   }
}
```

Compile Listing 4-2 (javac ExceptionThread.java) and run the resulting application (java ExceptionThread). You should observe this output:

```
Caught throwable java.lang.ArithmeticException: / by zero for thread
Thread[Thread-0,5,main]
```

You will not also see the default uncaught exception handler's output because the default handler isn't called. To see that output, you must comment out thd.setUncaught ExceptionHandler(uceh);. If you also comment out thd.setDefaultUncaughtException Handler(uceh);, you will see Listing 4-1's output.

Thread-Local Variables

You will sometimes want to associate per-thread data (such a user ID) with a thread. Although you can accomplish this task with a local variable, you can only do so while the local variable exists. You could use an instance field to keep this data around longer, but then you would have to deal with synchronization. Thankfully, Java supplies the java. lang.ThreadLocal class as a simple (and very handy) alternative.

Each ThreadLocal instance describes a *thread-local variable*, which is a variable that provides a separate storage slot to each thread that accesses the variable. You can think of a thread-local variable as a multislot variable in which each thread can store a different value in the same variable. Each thread sees only its value and is unaware of other threads having their own values in this variable.

ThreadLocal is generically declared as ThreadLocal<T>, where T identifies the type of value that is stored in the variable. This class declares the following constructor and methods:

- ThreadLocal(): Create a new thread-local variable.

- T get(): Return the value in the calling thread's storage slot. If an entry doesn't exist when the thread calls this method, get() calls initialValue().

- T initialValue(): Create the calling thread's storage slot and store an initial (default) value in this slot. The initial value defaults to null. You must subclass ThreadLocal and override this protected method to provide a more suitable initial value.

- void remove(): Remove the calling thread's storage slot. If this method is followed by get() with no intervening set(), get() calls initialValue().

- void set(T value): Set the value of the calling thread's storage slot to value.

Listing 4-3 shows how to use ThreadLocal to associate different user IDs with two threads.

Listing 4-3. Different User IDs for Different Threads

```
public class ThreadLocalDemo
{
    private static volatile ThreadLocal<String> userID =
        new ThreadLocal<String>();

    public static void main(String[] args)
    {
        Runnable r = new Runnable()
                     {
                         @Override
                         public void run()
                         {
                             String name = Thread.currentThread().getName();
                             if (name.equals("A"))
                                 userID.set("foxtrot");
                             else
                                 userID.set("charlie");
                             System.out.println(name + " " + userID.get());
                         }
                     };
        Thread thdA = new Thread(r);
        thdA.setName("A");
        Thread thdB = new Thread(r);
        thdB.setName("B");
        thdA.start();
        thdB.start();
    }
}
```

After instantiating ThreadLocal and assigning the reference to a volatile class field named userID (the field is volatile because it's accessed by different threads, which might execute on a multiprocessor/multicore machine—I could have specified final instead), the default main thread creates two more threads that store different java.lang.String objects in userID and output their objects.

Compile Listing 4-3 as follows:

```
javac ThreadLocalDemo.java
```

Run the resulting application as follows:

```
java ThreadLocalDemo
```

You should observe the following output (possibly not in this order):

```
A foxtrot
B charlie
```

Values stored in thread-local variables are not related. When a new thread is created, it gets a new storage slot containing initialValue()'s value. Perhaps you would prefer to pass a value from a *parent thread*, a thread that creates another thread, to a *child thread*, the created thread. You accomplish this task with InheritableThreadLocal.

InheritableThreadLocal is a subclass of ThreadLocal. As well as declaring an InheritableThreadLocal() constructor, this class declares the following protected method:

- T childValue(T parentValue): Calculate the child's initial value as a function of the parent's value at the time the child thread is created. This method is called from the parent thread before the child thread is started. The method returns the argument passed to parentValue and should be overridden when another value is desired.

Listing 4-4 shows how to use InheritableThreadLocal to pass a parent thread's Integer object to a child thread.

Listing 4-4. Passing an Object from a Parent Thread to a Child Thread

```java
public class InheritableThreadLocalDemo
{
    private static final InheritableThreadLocal<Integer> intVal =
        new InheritableThreadLocal<Integer>();

    public static void main(String[] args)
    {
        Runnable rP = () ->
                      {
                          intVal.set(new Integer(10));
                          Runnable rC = () ->
                                        {
                                            Thread thd = Thread.currentThread();
                                            String name = thd.getName();
                                            System.out.printf("%s %d%n", name,
                                                                intVal.get());
                                        };
                          Thread thdChild = new Thread(rC);
                          thdChild.setName("Child");
                          thdChild.start();
                      };
        new Thread(rP).start();
    }
}
```

After instantiating InheritableThreadLocal and assigning it to a final class field (I could have used volatile instead) named intVal, the default main thread creates a parent thread, which stores a java.lang.Integer object containing 10 in intVal. The parent thread creates a child thread, which accesses intVal and retrieves its parent thread's Integer object.

Compile Listing 4-4 as follows:

```
javac InheritableThreadLocalDemo.java
```

Run the resulting application as follows:

```
java InheritableThreadLocalDemo
```

You should observe the following output:

```
Child 10
```

■ **Note**   For more insight into ThreadLocal and how it's implemented, check out Patson Luk's "A Painless Introduction to Java's ThreadLocal Storage" blog post (http://java.dzone.com/articles/painless-introduction-javas-threadlocal-storage).

Timer Framework

It's often necessary to schedule a *task* (a unit of work) for *one-shot execution* (the task runs only once) or for repeated execution at regular intervals. For example, you might schedule an alarm clock task to run only once (perhaps to wake you up in the morning) or schedule a nightly backup task to run at regular intervals. With either kind of task, you might want the task to run at a specific time in the future or after an initial delay.

You can use Thread and related types to build a framework that accomplishes task scheduling. However, Java 1.3 introduced a more convenient and simpler alternative in the form of the java.util.Timer and java.util.TimerTask classes.

Timer lets you schedule TimerTasks for future execution (in a sequential manner) on a background thread, which is known as the *task-execution thread*. Timer tasks may be scheduled for one-shot execution or for repeated execution at regular intervals.

Listing 4-5 presents an application that demonstrates one-shot execution of a timer task.

Listing 4-5. Demonstrating One-Shot Execution

```java
import java.util.Timer;
import java.util.TimerTask;

public class TimerDemo
{
   public static void main(String[] args)
   {
      TimerTask task = new TimerTask()
                       {
                          @Override
                          public void run()
                          {
                             System.out.println("alarm going off");
                             System.exit(0);
                          }
                       };
      Timer timer = new Timer();
      timer.schedule(task, 2000); // Execute one-shot timer task after
                                  // 2-second delay.
   }
}
```

Listing 4-5 describes an application whose default main thread first instantiates a TimerTask anonymous subclass, whose overriding run() method outputs an alarm message, and then executes System.exit(0); because the application won't terminate until the nondaemon task-execution thread terminates. The default main thread then instantiates Timer and invokes its schedule() method with this task as the first argument. The second argument schedules this task for one-shot execution after an initial delay of 2000 milliseconds.

Compile Listing 4-5 as follows:

```
javac TimerDemo.java
```

Run the resulting application as follows:

```
java TimerDemo
```

You should observe output that's similar to the following output:

```
alarm going off
```

Listing 4-6 presents an application that demonstrates repeated execution at regular intervals of a timer task.

Listing 4-6. Displaying the Current Millisecond Value at Approximately One-Second Intervals

```
import java.util.Timer;
import java.util.TimerTask;

public class TimerDemo
{
   public static void main(String[] args)
   {
      TimerTask task = new TimerTask()
                       {
                           @Override
                           public void run()
                           {
                               System.out.println(System.currentTimeMillis());
                           }
                       };
      Timer timer = new Timer();
      timer.schedule(task, 0, 1000);
   }
}
```

Listing 4-6 describes an application whose default main thread first instantiates a TimerTask anonymous subclass, whose overriding run() method outputs the current time (in milliseconds). The default main thread then instantiates Timer and invokes its schedule() method with this task as the first argument. The second and third arguments schedule this task for repeated execution after no initial delay and every 1000 milliseconds.

Compile Listing 4-6 (javac TimerDemo.java) and run the resulting application (java TimerDemo). You should observe the truncated output here:

```
1445655847902
1445655848902
1445655849902
1445655850902
1445655851902
1445655852902
```

Timer in Depth

The previous applications ran their tasks on a nondaemon task-execution thread. Also, one task ran as a one-shot task, whereas the other task ran repeatedly. To understand how these choices were made, you need to learn more about Timer.

■ **Note**   Timer scales to large numbers of concurrently scheduled timer tasks (thousands of tasks should present no problem). Internally, this class uses a *binary heap* to represent its timer task queue so that the cost to schedule a timer task is $O(log\ n)$, where n is the number of concurrently scheduled timer tasks. To learn more about the $O()$ notation, check out Wikipedia's "Big O notation" topic (http://en.wikipedia.org/wiki/Big_O_notation).

Timer declares the following constructors:

- Timer(): Create a new timer whose task-execution thread doesn't run as a daemon thread.

- Timer(boolean isDaemon): Create a new timer whose task-execution thread may be specified to run as a daemon (pass true to isDaemon). A daemon thread is called for scenarios where the timer will be used to schedule repeating "maintenance activities," which must be performed for as long as the application is running, but shouldn't prolong the application's lifetime.

- Timer(String name): Create a new timer whose task-execution thread has the specified name. The task-execution thread doesn't run as a daemon thread. This constructor throws java.lang. NullPointerException when name is null.

- Timer(String name, boolean isDaemon): Create a new timer whose task-execution thread has the specified name and which may run as a daemon thread. This constructor throws NullPointerException when name is null.

Timer also declares the following methods:

- void cancel(): Terminate this timer, discarding any currently scheduled timer tasks. This method doesn't interfere with a currently executing timer task (when it exists). After a timer has been terminated, its execution thread terminates gracefully and no more timer tasks may be scheduled on it. (Calling cancel() from within the run() method of a timer task that was invoked by this timer absolutely guarantees that the ongoing task execution is the last task execution that will ever be performed by this timer.) This method may be called repeatedly; the second and subsequent calls have no effect.

- int purge(): Remove all canceled timer tasks from this timer's queue and return the number of timer tasks that have been removed. Calling purge() has no effect on the behavior of the timer, but eliminates references to the canceled timer tasks from the queue. When there are no external references to these timer tasks, they become eligible for garbage collection. (Most applications won't need to call this method, which is designed for use by the rare application that cancels a large number of timer tasks. Calling purge() trades time for space: this method's runtime may be proportional to $n + c * \log n$, where n is the number of timer tasks in the queue and c is the number of canceled timer tasks.) It's permissible to call purge() from within a timer task scheduled on this timer.

- void schedule(TimerTask task, Date time): Schedule task for execution at time. When time is in the past, task is scheduled for immediate execution. This method throws java.lang.IllegalArgumentException when time.getTime() is negative; java.lang.IllegalStateException when task was already scheduled or canceled, the timer was canceled, or the task-execution thread terminated; and NullPointerException when task or time is null.

- void schedule(TimerTask task, Date firstTime, long period): Schedule task for repeated fixed-delay execution, beginning at firstTime. Subsequent executions take place at approximately regular intervals, separated by period milliseconds. In *fixed-delay execution*, each execution is scheduled relative to the actual execution time of the previous execution. When an execution is delayed for any reason (such as garbage collection), subsequent executions are also delayed. In the long run, the frequency of execution will generally be slightly lower than the reciprocal of period (assuming the system clock underlying Object.wait(long) is accurate). As a consequence, when the scheduled firstTime value is in the past, task is scheduled for immediate execution. Fixed-delay execution is appropriate for recurring tasks that require "smoothness." In other words, this form of execution is appropriate for tasks where it's more important to keep the frequency accurate in the short run than in the long run. This includes most animation tasks, such as blinking a cursor at regular intervals. It also includes tasks wherein regular activity is performed in response to human input, such as automatically repeating a character for as long as a key is held down. This method throws IllegalArgumentException when firstTime.getTime() is negative or period is negative or zero; IllegalStateException when task was already scheduled or canceled, the timer was canceled, or the task-execution thread terminated; and NullPointerException when task or firstTime is null.

- void schedule(TimerTask task, long delay): Schedule task for execution after delay milliseconds. This method throws IllegalArgumentException when delay is negative or delay + System.currentTimeMillis() is negative; IllegalStateException when task was already scheduled or canceled, the timer was canceled, or the task-execution thread terminated; and NullPointerException when task is null.

- void schedule(TimerTask task, long delay, long period): Schedule task for repeated fixed-delay execution, beginning after delay milliseconds. Subsequent executions take place at approximately regular intervals separated by period milliseconds. This method throws IllegalArgumentException when delay is negative, delay + System.currentTimeMillis() is negative, or period is negative or zero; IllegalStateException when task was already scheduled or canceled, the timer was canceled, or the task-execution thread terminated; and NullPointerException when task is null.

- void scheduleAtFixedRate(TimerTask task, Date firstTime, long period): Schedule task for repeated fixed-rate execution, beginning at time. Subsequent executions take place at approximately regular intervals, separated by period milliseconds. In *fixed-rate execution*, each execution is scheduled relative to the scheduled execution time of the initial execution. When an execution is delayed for any reason (such as garbage collection), two or more executions will occur in rapid succession to "catch up." In the long run, the frequency of execution will be exactly the reciprocal of period (assuming the system clock underlying Object.wait(long) is accurate). As a consequence, when the scheduled firstTime is in the past, any "missed" executions will be scheduled for immediate "catch up" execution. Fixed-rate execution is appropriate for recurring activities that are sensitive to absolute time (such as ringing a chime every hour on the hour, or running scheduled maintenance every day at a particular time). It's also appropriate for recurring activities where the total time to perform a fixed number of executions is important, such as a countdown timer that ticks once every second for 10 seconds. Finally, fixed-rate execution is appropriate for scheduling multiple repeating timer tasks that must remain synchronized with respect to one another. This method throws IllegalArgumentException when firstTime.getTime() is negative, or period is negative or zero; IllegalStateException when task was already scheduled or canceled, the timer was canceled, or the task-execution thread terminated; and NullPointerException when task or firstTime is null.

- void scheduleAtFixedRate(TimerTask task, long delay, long period): Schedule task for repeated fixed-rate execution, beginning after delay milliseconds. Subsequent executions take place at approximately regular intervals, separated by period milliseconds. This method throws IllegalArgumentException when delay is negative, delay + System.currentTimeMillis() is negative, or period is negative or zero; IllegalStateException when task was already scheduled or canceled, the timer was canceled, or the task-execution thread terminated; and NullPointerException when task is null.

After the last live reference to a Timer object goes away and all outstanding timer tasks have completed execution, the timer's task-execution thread terminates gracefully (and becomes subject to garbage collection). However, this can take arbitrarily long to occur. (By default, the task-execution thread doesn't run as a daemon thread, so it's capable of preventing an application from terminating.) When an application wants to terminate a timer's task-execution thread rapidly, the application should invoke Timer's cancel() method.

When the timer's task-execution thread terminates unexpectedly, for example, because its stop() method was invoked (you should never call any of Thread's stop() methods because they're inherently unsafe), any further attempt to schedule a timer task on the timer results in IllegalStateException, as if Timer's cancel() method had been invoked.

TimerTask in Depth

Timer tasks are instances of classes that subclass the abstract TimerTask class, which implements the Runnable interface. When subclassing TimerTask, you override its void run() method to supply the timer task's code.

■ **Note**   Timer tasks should complete quickly. When a timer task takes too long to complete, it "hogs" the timer's task-execution thread, delaying the execution of subsequent timer tasks, which may "bunch up" and execute in rapid succession if and when the offending timer task finally completes.

You can also call the following methods from within the overriding timer task's run() method:

- boolean cancel(): Cancel this timer task. When the timer task has been scheduled for one-shot execution and hasn't yet run or when it hasn't yet been scheduled, it will never run. When the timer task has been scheduled for repeated execution, it will never run again. (When the timer task is running when this call occurs, the timer task will run to completion, but will never run again.) Calling cancel() from within the run() method of a repeating timer task absolutely guarantees that the timer task won't run again. This method may be called repeatedly; the second and subsequent calls have no effect. This method returns true when this timer task is scheduled for one-shot execution and hasn't yet run or when this timer task is scheduled for repeated execution. It returns false when the timer task was scheduled for one-shot execution and has already run, when the timer task was never scheduled, or when the timer task was already canceled. (Loosely speaking, this method returns true when it prevents one or more scheduled executions from taking place.)

- `long scheduledExecutionTime()`: Return the scheduled execution time of the most recent actual execution of this timer task. (When this method is invoked while timer task execution is in progress, the return value is the scheduled execution time of the ongoing timer task execution.) This method is typically invoked from within a task's `run()` method to determine whether the current execution of the timer task is sufficiently timely to warrant performing the scheduled activity. For example, you would specify code similar to `if (System.currentTimeMillis() -scheduledExecutionTime() >= MAX_TARDINESS) return;` at the start of the `run()` method to abort the current timer task execution when it's not timely. This method is typically not used in conjunction with fixed-delay execution repeating timer tasks because their scheduled execution times are allowed to drift over time and are thus not terribly significant. `scheduledExecutionTime()` returns the time at which the most recent execution of this timer task was scheduled to occur, in the format returned by `java.util.Date.getTime()`. The return value is undefined when the timer task has yet to commence its first execution.

EXERCISES

The following exercises are designed to test your understanding of Chapter 4's content:

1. Define thread group.

2. Why might you use a thread group?

3. Why should you avoid using thread groups?

4. Why should you be aware of thread groups?

5. Define thread-local variable.

6. True or false: If an entry doesn't exist in the calling thread's storage slot when the thread calls `get()`, this method calls `initialValue()`.

7. How would you pass a value from a parent thread to a child thread?

8. Identify the classes that form the Timer Framework.

9. True or false: `Timer()` creates a new timer whose task-execution thread runs as a daemon thread.

10. Define fixed-delay execution.

11. Which methods do you call to schedule a task for fixed-delay execution?

12. Define fixed-rate execution.

13. What is the difference between Timer's cancel() method and TimerTask's cancel() method?

14. Create a BackAndForth application that uses Timer and TimerTask to repeatedly move an asterisk forward 20 steps and then backward 20 steps. The asterisk is output via System. out.print().

Summary

The ThreadGroup class describes a thread group, which stores a set of threads. It simplifies thread management by applying method calls to all contained threads. You should avoid using thread groups because the most useful methods are deprecated and because of a race condition.

The ThreadLocal class describes a thread-local variable, which lets you associate per-thread data (such as a user ID) with a thread. It provides a separate storage slot to each thread that accesses the variable. Think of a thread-local variable as a multislot variable in which each thread can store a different value in the same variable. Each thread sees only its value and is unaware of other threads having their own values in this variable. Values stored in thread-local variables are not related. A parent thread can use the InheritableThreadLocal class to pass a value to a child thread.

It's often necessary to schedule a task for one-shot execution or for repeated execution at regular intervals. Java 1.3 introduced the Timer Framework, which consists of Timer and TimerTask classes, to facilitate working with threads in a timer context.

Chapter 5 introduces the concurrency utilities and presents executors.

PART II

Concurrency Utilities

■ ■ ■

Concurrency Utilities and Executors

The previous four chapters focused on Java's low-level support for threads. This chapter switches that focus to Java's high-level thread support, which is known as the concurrency utilities. Think of the concurrency utilities as being analogous to writing applications in a high-level language and its low-level thread support as being analogous to writing applications in assembly language. After briefly introducing you to these utilities, I take you on a tour of executors. The next three chapters will cover other subsets of the various concurrency utilities.

Introducing the Concurrency Utilities

Java's low-level threads support lets you create multithreaded applications that offer better performance and responsiveness over their single-threaded counterparts. However, there are problems:

- Low-level concurrency primitives such as synchronized and wait()/notify() are often hard to use correctly. Incorrect use of these primitives can result in race conditions, thread starvation, deadlock, and other hazards, which can be hard to detect and debug.

- Too much reliance on the synchronized primitive can lead to performance issues, which affect an application's *scalability*. This is a significant problem for highly-threaded applications such as web servers.

- Developers often need higher-level constructs such as thread pools and semaphores. Because these constructs aren't included with Java's low-level thread support, developers have been forced to build their own, which is a time-consuming and error-prone activity.

To address these problems, Java 5 introduced the *concurrency utilities*, a powerful and extensible framework of high-performance threading utilities such as thread pools and blocking queues. This framework consists of various types in the following packages:

- `java.util.concurrent`: Utility types that are often used in concurrent programming, for example, executors.

- `java.util.concurrent.atomic`: Utility classes that support lock-free thread-safe programming on single variables.

- `java.util.concurrent.locks`: Utility types that lock and wait on *conditions* (objects that let threads suspend execution [wait] until notified by other threads that some boolean state may now be true). Locking and waiting via these types is more performant and flexible than doing so via Java's monitor-based synchronization and wait/notification mechanisms.

This framework also introduces a `long nanoTime()` method to the `java.lang.System` class, which lets you access a nanosecond-granularity time source for making relative time measurements.

The concurrency utilities can be classified as executors, synchronizers, a locking framework, and more. I explore executors in the next section and these other categories in subsequent chapters.

Exploring Executors

The Threads API lets you execute runnable tasks via expressions such as `new java.lang.Thread(new RunnableTask()).start();`. These expressions tightly couple task submission with the task's execution mechanics (run on the current thread, a new thread, or a thread arbitrarily chosen from a *pool* [group] of threads).

■ **Note** A *task* is an object whose class implements the `java.lang.Runnable` interface (a runnable task) or the `java.util.concurrent.Callable` interface (a callable task). I'll say more about `Callable` later in this chapter.

The concurrency utilities include executors as a high-level alternative to low-level thread expressions for executing runnable tasks. An *executor* is an object whose class directly or indirectly implements the `java.util.concurrent.Executor` interface, which decouples task submission from task-execution mechanics.

■ **Note**   The Executor Framework's use of interfaces to decouple task submission from task-execution is analogous to the Collections Framework's use of core interfaces to decouple lists, sets, queues, and maps from their implementations. Decoupling results in flexible code that's easier to maintain.

Executor declares a solitary void execute(Runnable runnable) method that executes the runnable task named runnable at some point in the future. execute() throws java.lang.NullPointerException when runnable is null and java.util. concurrent.RejectedExecutionException when it cannot execute runnable.

■ **Note**   RejectedExecutionException can be thrown when an executor is shutting down and doesn't want to accept new tasks. Also, this exception can be thrown when the executor doesn't have enough room to store the task (perhaps the executor uses a bounded blocking queue to store tasks and the queue is full—I discuss blocking queues in Chapter 8).

The following example presents the Executor equivalent of the aforementioned new Thread(new RunnableTask()).start(); expression:

```
Executor executor = ...; //  ... represents some executor creation
executor.execute(new RunnableTask());
```

Although Executor is easy to use, this interface is limited in various ways:

- Executor focuses exclusively on Runnable. Because Runnable's run() method doesn't return a value, there's no easy way for a runnable task to return a value to its caller.

- Executor doesn't provide a way to track the progress of runnable tasks that are executing, cancel an executing runnable task, or determine when the runnable task finishes execution.

- Executor cannot execute a collection of runnable tasks.

- Executor doesn't provide a way for an application to shut down an executor (much less properly shut down an executor).

These limitations are addressed by the java.util.concurrent.ExecutorService interface, which extends Executor and whose implementation is typically a thread pool. Table 5-1 describes ExecutorService's methods.

Table 5-1. *ExecutorService's Methods*

Method	Description
`boolean awaitTermination(long timeout, TimeUnit unit)`	Block (wait) until all tasks have finished after a shutdown request, the `timeout` (measured in unit time units) expires, or the current thread is interrupted, whichever happens first. Return `true` when this executor has terminated and `false` when the `timeout` elapses before termination. This method throws `java.lang.InterruptedException` when interrupted.
`<T> List<Future<T>> invokeAll(Collection<? extends Callable<T>> tasks)`	Execute each callable task in the `tasks` collection and return a `java.util.List` of `java.util.concurrent.Future` instances (discussed later in this chapter) that hold task statuses and results when all tasks complete—a task completes through normal termination or by throwing an exception. The `List` of `Future`s is in the same sequential order as the sequence of tasks returned by `tasks`' iterator. This method throws `InterruptedException` when it's interrupted while waiting, in which case unfinished tasks are canceled; `NullPointerException` when `tasks` or any of its elements is `null`; and `RejectedExecutionException` when any one of `tasks`' tasks cannot be scheduled for execution.
`<T> List<Future<T>> invokeAll(Collection<? extends Callable<T>> tasks, long timeout, TimeUnit unit)`	Execute each callable task in the `tasks` collection and return a `List` of `Future` instances that hold task statuses and results when all tasks complete—a task completes through normal termination or by throwing an exception—or the `timeout` (measured in unit time units) expires. Tasks that are not completed at expiry are canceled. The `List` of `Future`s is in the same sequential order as the sequence of tasks returned by `tasks`' iterator. This method throws `InterruptedException` when it's interrupted while waiting (unfinished tasks are canceled). It also throws `NullPointerException` when `tasks`, any of its elements, or `unit` is `null`; and throws `RejectedExecutionException` when any one of `tasks`' tasks cannot be scheduled for execution.

(continued)

Table 5-1. (*continued*)

Method	Description
`<T> T invokeAny(Collection<? extends Callable<T>> tasks)`	Execute the given `tasks`, returning the result of an arbitrary task that's completed successfully (in other words, without throwing an exception), if any does. On normal or exceptional return, tasks that haven't completed are canceled. This method throws `InterruptedException` when it's interrupted while waiting, `NullPointerException` when `tasks` or any of its elements is `null`, `java.lang.IllegalArgumentException` when `tasks` is empty, `java.util.concurrent.ExecutionException` when no task completes successfully, and `RejectedExecutionException` when none of the tasks can be scheduled for execution.
`<T> T invokeAny(Collection<? extends Callable<T>> tasks, long timeout, TimeUnit unit)`	Execute the given `tasks`, returning the result of an arbitrary task that's completed successfully (no exception was thrown), if any does before the timeout (measured in `unit` time units) expires—tasks that are not completed at expiry are canceled. On normal or exceptional return, tasks that have not completed are canceled. This method throws `InterruptedException` when it's interrupted while waiting; `NullPointerException` when `tasks`, any of its elements, or `unit` is `null`; `IllegalArgumentException` when `tasks` is empty; `java.util.concurrent.TimeoutException` when the `timeout` elapses before any task successfully completes; `ExecutionException` when no task completes successfully; and `RejectedExecutionException` when none of the tasks can be scheduled for execution.
`boolean isShutdown()`	Return `true` when this executor has been shut down; otherwise, return `false`.
`boolean isTerminated()`	Return `true` when all tasks have completed following shutdown; otherwise, return `false`. This method will never return `true` prior to `shutdown()` or `shutdownNow()` being called.
`void shutdown()`	Initiate an orderly shutdown in which previously submitted tasks are executed, but no new tasks will be accepted. Calling this method has no effect after the executor has shut down. This method doesn't wait for previously submitted tasks to complete execution. Use `awaitTermination()` when waiting is necessary.

(*continued*)

Table 5-1. (*continued*)

Method	Description
`List<Runnable> shutdownNow()`	Attempt to stop all actively executing tasks, halt the processing of waiting tasks, and return a list of the tasks that were awaiting execution. There are no guarantees beyond best-effort attempts to stop processing actively executing tasks. For example, typical implementations will cancel via `Thread.interrupt()`, so any task that fails to respond to interrupts may never terminate.
`<T> Future<T> submit(Callable<T> task)`	Submit a callable task for execution and return a `Future` instance representing task's pending results. The `Future` instance's `get()` method returns task's result on successful completion. This method throws `RejectedExecutionException` when task cannot be scheduled for execution and `NullPointerException` when task is `null`. If you would like to immediately block while waiting for a task to complete, you can use constructions of the form `result = exec.submit(aCallable).get();`.
`Future<?> submit(Runnable task)`	Submit a runnable task for execution and return a `Future` instance representing task's pending results. The `Future` instance's `get()` method returns task's result on successful completion. This method throws `RejectedExecutionException` when task cannot be scheduled for execution and `NullPointerException` when task is `null`.
`<T> Future<T> submit(Runnable task, T result)`	Submit a runnable task for execution and return a `Future` instance whose `get()` method returns result's value on successful completion. This method throws `RejectedExecutionException` when task cannot be scheduled for execution and `NullPointerException` when task is `null`.

Table 5-1 refers to `java.util.concurrent.TimeUnit`, an enum that represents time durations at given units of granularity: DAYS, HOURS, MICROSECONDS, MILLISECONDS, MINUTES, NANOSECONDS, and SECONDS. Furthermore, `TimeUnit` declares methods for converting across units (such as `long toHours(long duration)`), and for performing timing and delay operations (such as `void sleep(long timeout)`) in these units.

Table 5-1 also refers to *callable tasks*. Unlike Runnable, whose `void run()` method cannot return a value and throw checked exceptions, `Callable<V>`'s V `call()` method returns a value and can throw checked exceptions because it's declared with a `throws Exception` clause.

Finally, Table 5-1 refers to the Future interface, which represents the result of an asynchronous computation. The result is known as a *future* because it typically will not be available until some moment in the future. Future, whose generic type is Future<V>, provides methods for canceling a task, for returning a task's value, and for determining whether or not the task has finished. Table 5-2 describes Future's methods.

Table 5-2. *Future's Methods*

Method	Description
boolean cancel(boolean mayInterruptIfRunning)	Attempt to cancel execution of this task and return true when the task is canceled; otherwise, return false (the task may have completed normally before cancel() was called). Cancellation fails when the task is done, canceled, or couldn't be canceled for another reason. If successful and this task hadn't yet started, the task should never run. If the task has started, mayInterruptIfRunning determines whether (true) or not (false) the thread running this task should be interrupted in an attempt to stop the task. After returning, subsequent calls to isDone() always return true; isCancelled() always return true when cancel() returns true.
V get()	Wait if necessary for the task to complete and then return the result. This method throws java.util.concurrent. CancellationException when the task was canceled prior to this method being called, ExecutionException when the task threw an exception, and InterruptedException when the current thread was interrupted while waiting.
V get(long timeout, TimeUnit unit)	Wait at most timeout units (as specified by unit) for the task to complete and then return the result (if available). This method throws CancellationException when the task was canceled prior to this method being called, ExecutionException when the task threw an exception, InterruptedException when the current thread was interrupted while waiting, and TimeoutException when this method's timeout value expires (the wait times out).
boolean isCancelled()	Return true when this task was canceled before it completed normally; otherwise, return false.
boolean isDone()	Return true when this task completed; otherwise, return false. Completion may be due to normal termination, an exception, or cancellation—this method returns true in all of these cases.

Suppose you intend to write an application whose graphical user interface lets the user enter a word. After the user enters the word, the application presents this word to several online dictionaries and obtains each dictionary's entry. These entries are subsequently displayed to the user.

Because online access can be slow, and because the user interface should remain responsive (perhaps the user might want to end the application), you offload the "obtain word entries" task to an executor that runs this task on a separate thread. The following example uses ExecutorService, Callable, and Future to accomplish this objective:

```
ExecutorService executor = ...; // ... represents some executor creation
Future<String[]> taskFuture =
   executor.submit(new Callable<String[]>()
                  {
                     @Override
                     public String[] call()
                     {
                        String[] entries = ...;
                        // Access online dictionaries
                        // with search word and populate
                        // entries with their resulting
                        // entries.
                        return entries;
                     }
                  });
// Do stuff.
String entries = taskFuture.get();
```

After obtaining an executor in some manner (you will learn how shortly), the example's thread submits a callable task to the executor. The submit() method immediately returns with a reference to a Future object for controlling task execution and accessing results. The thread ultimately calls this object's get() method to get these results.

■ **Note** The java.util.concurrent.ScheduledExecutorService interface extends ExecutorService and describes an executor that lets you schedule tasks to run once or to execute periodically after a given delay.

Although you could create your own Executor, ExecutorService, and ScheduledExecutorService implementations (such as class DirectExecutor implements Executor { @Override public void execute(Runnable r) { r.run(); } }— run executor directly on the calling thread), there's a simpler alternative: java.util. concurrent.Executors.

■ **Tip** If you intend to create your own `ExecutorService` implementations, you will find it helpful to work with the `java.util.concurrent.AbstractExecutorService` and `java.util.concurrent.FutureTask` classes.

The `Executors` utility class declares several class methods that return instances of various `ExecutorService` and `ScheduledExecutorService` implementations (and other kinds of instances). This class's `static` methods accomplish the following tasks:

- Create and return an `ExecutorService` instance that's configured with commonly used configuration settings.

- Create and return a `ScheduledExecutorService` instance that's configured with commonly used configuration settings.

- Create and return a "wrapped" `ExecutorService` or `ScheduledExecutorService` instance that disables reconfiguration of the executor service by making implementation-specific methods inaccessible.

- Create and return a `java.util.concurrent.ThreadFactory` instance (that is, an instance of a class that implements the `ThreadFactory` interface) for creating new `Thread` objects.

- Create and return a `Callable` instance out of other closure-like forms so that it can be used in execution methods that require `Callable` arguments (such as `ExecutorService`'s `submit(Callable)` method). Wikipedia's "Closure (computer science)" entry at `http://en.wikipedia.org/wiki/Closure_(computer_science)` introduces the topic of closures.

For example, `static ExecutorService newFixedThreadPool(int nThreads)` creates a thread pool that reuses a fixed number of threads operating off of a shared unbounded queue. At most, nThreads threads are actively processing tasks. If additional tasks are submitted when all threads are active, they wait in the queue for an available thread.

If any thread terminates because of a failure during execution before the executor shuts down, a new thread will take its place when needed to execute subsequent tasks. The threads in the pool will exist until the executor is explicitly shut down. This method throws `IllegalArgumentException` when you pass zero or a negative value to nThreads.

■ **Note** Thread pools are used to eliminate the overhead from having to create a new thread for each submitted task. Thread creation isn't cheap, and having to create many threads could severely impact an application's performance.

You would commonly use executors, runnables, callables, and futures in file and network input/output contexts. Performing a lengthy calculation offers another scenario where you could use these types. For example, Listing 5-1 uses an executor, a callable, and a future in a calculation context of Euler's number e (2.71828...).

Listing 5-1. Calculating Euler's Number e

```java
import java.math.BigDecimal;
import java.math.MathContext;
import java.math.RoundingMode;

import java.util.concurrent.Callable;
import java.util.concurrent.ExecutionException;
import java.util.concurrent.ExecutorService;
import java.util.concurrent.Executors;
import java.util.concurrent.Future;

public class CalculateE
{
   final static int LASTITER = 17;

   public static void main(String[] args)
   {
      ExecutorService executor = Executors.newFixedThreadPool(1);
      Callable<BigDecimal> callable;
      callable = new Callable<BigDecimal>()
                 {
                     @Override
                     public BigDecimal call()
                     {
                        MathContext mc =
                           new MathContext(100, RoundingMode.HALF_UP);
                        BigDecimal result = BigDecimal.ZERO;
                        for (int i = 0; i <= LASTITER; i++)
                        {
                           BigDecimal factorial =
                              factorial(new BigDecimal(i));
                           BigDecimal res = BigDecimal.ONE.divide(factorial,
                                                                 mc);
                           result = result.add(res);
                        }
                        return result;
                     }
```

```
                   public BigDecimal factorial(BigDecimal n)
                   {
                       if (n.equals(BigDecimal.ZERO))
                           return BigDecimal.ONE;
                       else
                           return n.multiply(factorial(n.
                                         subtract(BigDecimal.ONE)));
                   }
               };
       Future<BigDecimal> taskFuture = executor.submit(callable);
       try
       {
          while (!taskFuture.isDone())
             System.out.println("waiting");
          System.out.println(taskFuture.get());
       }
       catch(ExecutionException ee)
       {
          System.err.println("task threw an exception");
          System.err.println(ee);
       }
       catch(InterruptedException ie)
       {
          System.err.println("interrupted while waiting");
       }
       executor.shutdownNow();
   }
}
```

The default main thread that executes main() first obtains an executor by calling
Executors' newFixedThreadPool() method. It then instantiates an anonymous class
that implements the Callable interface and submits this task to the executor, receiving a
Future instance in response.

After submitting a task, a thread typically does some other work until it requires the
task's result. I simulate this work by having the main thread repeatedly output a waiting
message until the Future instance's isDone() method returns true. (In a realistic
application, I would avoid this looping.) At this point, the main thread calls the instance's
get() method to obtain the result, which is then output. The main thread then shuts
down the executor.

■ **Caution**   It's important to shut down an executor after it completes; otherwise,
the application might not end. The previous executor accomplishes this task by calling
shutdownNow(). (You could also use the shutdown() method.)

The callable's `call()` method calculates e by evaluating the mathematical power series e = 1 / 0! + 1 / 1! + 1 / 2! + ... This series can be evaluated by summing 1 / $n!$, where n ranges from 0 to infinity (and ! stands for factorial).

`call()` first instantiates `java.math.MathContext` to encapsulate a *precision* (number of digits) and a rounding mode. I chose 100 as an upper limit on e's precision, and I also chose `HALF_UP` as the rounding mode.

■ **Tip** Increase the precision as well as the value of `LASTITER` to converge the series to a lengthier and more accurate approximation of e.

`call()` next initializes a `java.math.BigDecimal` local variable named `result` to `BigDecimal.ZERO`. It then enters a loop that calculates a factorial, divides `BigDecimal.ONE` by the factorial, and adds the division result to `result`.

The `divide()` method takes the `MathContext` instance as its second argument to provide rounding information. (If I specified 0 as the precision for the math context and a *nonterminating decimal expansion* [the quotient result of the division cannot be represented exactly—0.3333333..., for example] occurred, `java.lang.ArithmeticException` would be thrown to alert the caller to the fact that the quotient cannot be represented exactly. The executor would rethrow this exception as `ExecutionException`.)

Compile Listing 5-1 as follows:

```
javac CalculateE.java
```

Run the resulting application as follows:

```
java CalculateE
```

You should observe output that's similar to the following (you'll probably observe more `waiting` messages):

```
waiting
waiting
waiting
waiting
waiting
2.718281828459045070516047795848605061178979635251032698900735004065225042504250
48433140558879743442457417300394540627711
```

EXERCISES

The following exercises are designed to test your understanding of Chapter 5's content:

1. What are the concurrency utilities?

2. Identify the packages in which the concurrency utilities types are stored.

3. Define task.

4. Define executor.

5. Identify the Executor interface's limitations.

6. How are Executor's limitations overcome?

7. What differences exist between Runnable's run( ) method and Callable's call( ) method?

8. True or false: You can throw checked and unchecked exceptions from Runnable's run( ) method but can only throw unchecked exceptions from Callable's call( ) method.

9. Define future.

10. Describe the Executors class's newFixedThreadPool( ) method.

11. Refactor the following CountingThreads application to work with Executors and ExecutorService:

```java
public class CountingThreads
{
  public static void main(String[] args)
  {
    Runnable r = new Runnable()
          {
            @Override
            public void run()
            {
              String name = Thread.currentThread().
                          getName();
              int count = 0;
              while (true)
                System.out.println(name + ": " +
                                count++);
            }
          };
```

```
        Thread thdA = new Thread(r);
        Thread thdB = new Thread(r);
        thdA.start();
        thdB.start();
      }
    }
```

12. When you execute the previous exercise's CountingThreads application, you'll observe output that identifies the threads via names such as pool-1-thread-1. Modify CountingThreads so that you observe names A and B. Hint: You'll need to use ThreadFactory.

Summary

Java's low-level thread capabilities let you create multithreaded applications that offer better performance and responsiveness over their single-threaded counterparts. However, performance issues that affect an application's scalability and other problems resulted in Java 5's introduction of the concurrency utilities.

The concurrency utilities organize various types into three packages: java.util. concurrent, java.util.concurrent.atomic, and java.util.concurrent.locks. Basic types for executors, thread pools, concurrent hashmaps, and other high-level concurrency constructs are stored in java.util.concurrent; classes that support lock-free, thread-safe programming on single variables are stored in java.util.concurrent. atomic; and types for locking and waiting on conditions are stored in java.util. concurrent.locks.

An executor decouples task submission from task-execution mechanics and is described by the Executor, ExecutorService, and ScheduledExecutorService interfaces. You obtain an executor by calling one of the utility methods in the Executors class. Executors are associated with callables and futures.

Chapter 6 presents synchronizers.

CHAPTER 6

Synchronizers

Java provides the synchronized keyword for synchronizing thread access to critical sections. Because it can be difficult to correctly write synchronized code that's based on synchronized, high-level *synchronizers* (classes that facilitate common forms of synchronization) are included in the concurrency utilities. In this chapter, I introduce you to the countdown latch, cyclic barrier, exchanger, semaphore, and phaser synchronizers.

Countdown Latches

A *countdown latch* causes one or more threads to wait at a "gate" until another thread opens this gate, at which point these other threads can continue. It consists of a count and operations for "causing a thread to wait until the count reaches zero" and "decrementing the count."

The java.util.concurrent.CountDownLatch class implements the countdown latch synchronizer. You initialize a CountDownLatch instance to a specific count by invoking this class's CountDownLatch(int count) constructor, which throws java.lang.IllegalArgumentException when the value passed to count is negative.

CountDownLatch also offers the following methods:

- void await(): Force the calling thread to wait until the latch has counted down to zero, unless the thread is interrupted, in which case java.lang.InterruptedException is thrown. This method returns immediately when the count is zero.

- boolean await(long timeout, TimeUnit unit): Force the calling thread to wait until the latch has counted down to zero or the specified timeout value in unit time-units has expired, or the thread is interrupted, in which case InterruptedException is thrown. This method returns immediately when the count is zero. It returns true when the count reaches zero or false when the waiting time elapses.

- void countDown(): Decrement the count, releasing all waiting threads when the count reaches zero. Nothing happens when the count is already zero when this method is called.

- `long getCount()`: Return the current count. This method is useful for testing and debugging.

- `String toString()`: Return a string identifying this latch as well as its state. The state, in brackets, includes string literal `"Count ="` followed by the current count.

You'll often use a countdown latch to ensure that threads start working at approximately the same time. For example, check out Listing 6-1.

Listing 6-1. Using a Countdown Latch to Trigger a Coordinated Start

```
import java.util.concurrent.CountDownLatch;
import java.util.concurrent.ExecutorService;
import java.util.concurrent.Executors;

public class CountDownLatchDemo
{
   final static int NTHREADS = 3;

   public static void main(String[] args)
   {
      final CountDownLatch startSignal = new CountDownLatch(1);
      final CountDownLatch doneSignal = new CountDownLatch(NTHREADS);
      Runnable r = new Runnable()
                  {
                     @Override
                     public void run()
                     {
                        try
                        {
                           report("entered run()");
                           startSignal.await();  // wait until told to ...
                           report("doing work"); // ... proceed
                           Thread.sleep((int) (Math.random() * 1000));
                           doneSignal.countDown(); // reduce count on which
                                                   // main thread is ...
                        }                          // waiting
                        catch (InterruptedException ie)
                        {
                           System.err.println(ie);
                        }
                     }
```

```
              void report(String s)
              {
                  System.out.println(System.currentTimeMillis() +
                                   ": " + Thread.currentThread() +
                                   ": " + s);
              }
          };
      ExecutorService executor = Executors.newFixedThreadPool(NTHREADS);
      for (int i = 0; i < NTHREADS; i++)
         executor.execute(r);
      try
      {
         System.out.println("main thread doing something");
         Thread.sleep(1000); // sleep for 1 second
         startSignal.countDown(); // let all threads proceed
         System.out.println("main thread doing something else");
         doneSignal.await(); // wait for all threads to finish
         executor.shutdownNow();
      }
      catch (InterruptedException ie)
      {
         System.err.println(ie);
      }
   }
}
```

Listing 6-1's default main thread first creates a pair of countdown latches. The startSignal countdown latch prevents any worker thread from proceeding until the default main thread is ready for them to proceed. The doneSignal countdown latch causes the default main thread to wait until all worker threads have finished.

The default main thread next creates a runnable with a run() method that is executed by subsequently created worker threads.

run() first outputs a message and then calls startSignal's await() method to wait for this countdown latch's count to read zero before proceeding, at which point run() outputs a message that indicates work being done and sleeps for a random period of time (0 through 999 milliseconds) to simulate this work.

At this point, run() invokes doneSignal's countDown() method to decrement this latch's count. Once this count reaches zero, the default main thread waiting on this signal will continue, shutting down the executor and terminating the application.

After creating the runnable, the default main thread obtains an executor that's based on a thread pool of NTHREADS threads, and then calls the executor's execute() method NTHREADS times, passing the runnable to each of the NTHREADS pool-based threads. This action starts the worker threads, which enter run().

Next, the default main thread outputs a message and sleeps for one second to simulate doing additional work (giving all the worker threads a chance to have entered run() and invoke startSignal.await()), invokes startSignal's countDown() method to cause the worker threads to start running, outputs a message to indicate that it's doing something else, and invokes doneSignal's await() method to wait for this countdown latch's count to reach zero before it can proceed.

Compile Listing 6-1 as follows:

```
javac CountDownLatchDemo.java
```

Run the resulting application as follows:

```
java CountDownLatchDemo
```

You should observe output that's similar to the following (message order may differ somewhat):

```
main thread doing something
1445802274931: Thread[pool-1-thread-2,5,main]: entered run()
1445802274931: Thread[pool-1-thread-3,5,main]: entered run()
1445802274931: Thread[pool-1-thread-1,5,main]: entered run()
main thread doing something else
1445802275931: Thread[pool-1-thread-2,5,main]: doing work
1445802275931: Thread[pool-1-thread-3,5,main]: doing work
1445802275933: Thread[pool-1-thread-1,5,main]: doing work
```

Cyclic Barriers

A *cyclic barrier* lets a set of threads wait for each other to reach a common barrier point. The barrier is *cyclic* because it can be reused after the waiting threads are released. This synchronizer is useful in applications involving a fixed-size party of threads that must occasionally wait for each other.

The java.util.concurrent.CyclicBarrier class implements the cyclic barrier synchronizer. You initialize a CyclicBarrier instance to a specific number of *parties* (threads working toward a common goal) by invoking this class's CyclicBarrier(int parties) constructor. This constructor throws IllegalArgumentException when the value passed to parties is less than 1.

Alternatively, you can invoke the CyclicBarrier(int parties, Runnable barrierAction) constructor to initialize a cyclic barrier to a specific number of parties and a barrierAction that's executed when the barrier is *tripped*. In other words, when parties - 1 threads are waiting and one more thread arrives, the arriving thread executes barrierAction and then all threads proceed. This runnable is useful for updating shared state before any of the threads continue. This constructor throws IllegalArgumentException when the value passed to parties is less than 1. (The former constructor invokes this constructor passing null to barrierAction—no runnable will be executed when the barrier is tripped.)

CyclicBarrier also offers the following methods:

- int await():Force the calling thread to wait until all parties have invoked await() on this cyclic barrier. The calling thread will also stop waiting when it or another waiting thread is interrupted, another thread times out while waiting, or another thread invokes reset() on this cyclic barrier. If the calling thread has its interrupted status set on entry or is interrupted while waiting, this method throws InterruptedException and the calling thread's interrupted status is cleared. The method throws java.util. concurrent.BrokenBarrierException when the barrier is reset (via reset()) while any thread is waiting, or the barrier is broken when await() is invoked or while any thread is waiting. When any thread is interrupted while waiting, all other waiting threads throw BrokenBarrierException and the barrier is placed in the broken state. If the calling thread is the last thread to arrive and a non-null barrierAction was supplied in the constructor, the calling thread executes this runnable before allowing the other threads to continue. This method returns the arrival index of the calling thread, where index getParties() - 1 indicates the first thread to arrive and zero indicates the last thread to arrive.

- int await(long timeout, TimeUnit unit): This method is equivalent to the previous method except that it lets you specify how long the calling thread is willing to wait. This method throws java.util.concurrent.TimeoutException when this timeout expires while the thread is waiting.

- int getNumberWaiting(): Return the number of parties that are currently waiting at the barrier. This method is useful for debugging and in partnership with assertions.

- int getParties(): Return the number of parties that are required to trip the barrier.

- boolean isBroken(): Return true when one or more parties broke out of this barrier because of interruption or timeout since the cyclic barrier was constructed or the last reset, or when a barrier action failed because of an exception; otherwise, return false.

- void reset(): Reset the barrier to its initial state. If any parties are currently waiting at the barrier, they will return with a BrokenBarrierException. Note that resets after a breakage has occurred for other reasons can be complicated to carry out; threads need to resynchronize in some other way and choose one thread to perform the reset. Therefore, it might be preferable to create a new barrier for subsequent use.

Cyclic barriers are useful in *parallel decomposition* scenarios, where a lengthy task is divided into subtasks whose individual results are later merged into the overall result of the task. CyclicBarrier's Javadoc presents example code that's completed in Listing 6-2.

Listing 6-2. Using a Cyclic Barrier to Decompose a Task into Subtasks

```java
import java.util.concurrent.BrokenBarrierException;
import java.util.concurrent.CyclicBarrier;

public class CyclicBarrierDemo
{
   public static void main(String[] args)
   {
      float[][] matrix = new float[3][3];
      int counter = 0;
      for (int row = 0; row < matrix.length; row++)
         for (int col = 0; col < matrix[0].length; col++)
         matrix[row][col] = counter++;
      dump(matrix);
      System.out.println();
      Solver solver = new Solver(matrix);
      System.out.println();
      dump(matrix);
   }

   static void dump(float[][] matrix)
   {
      for (int row = 0; row < matrix.length; row++)
      {
         for (int col = 0; col < matrix[0].length; col++)
            System.out.print(matrix[row][col] + " ");
         System.out.println();
      }
   }
}

class Solver
{
   final int N;
   final float[][] data;
   final CyclicBarrier barrier;

   class Worker implements Runnable
   {
      int myRow;
      boolean done = false;

      Worker(int row)
      {
         myRow = row;
      }
```

```java
   boolean done()
   {
      return done;
   }

   void processRow(int myRow)
   {
      System.out.println("Processing row: " + myRow);
      for (int i = 0; i < N; i++)
         data[myRow][i] *= 10;
      done = true;
   }

   @Override
   public void run()
   {
      while (!done())
      {
         processRow(myRow);

         try
         {
            barrier.await();
         }
         catch (InterruptedException ie)
         {
            return;
         }
         catch (BrokenBarrierException bbe)
         {
            return;
         }
      }
   }
}

public Solver(float[][] matrix)
{
   data = matrix;
   N = matrix.length;
   barrier = new CyclicBarrier(N,
                                 new Runnable()
                                 {
                                    @Override
                                    public void run()
                                    {
                                       mergeRows();
                                    }
                                 });
```

```
        for (int i = 0; i < N; ++i)
            new Thread(new Worker(i)).start();

        waitUntilDone();
    }

    void mergeRows()
    {
        System.out.println("merging");
        synchronized("abc")
        {
            "abc".notify();
        }
    }

    void waitUntilDone()
    {
        synchronized("abc")
        {
            try
            {
                System.out.println("main thread waiting");
                "abc".wait();
                System.out.println("main thread notified");
            }
            catch (InterruptedException ie)
            {
                System.out.println("main thread interrupted");
            }
        }
    }
}
```

Listing 6-2's default main thread first creates a square matrix of floating-point values and dumps this matrix to the standard output stream. This thread then instantiates the Solver class, which creates a separate thread for performing a calculation on each row. The modified matrix is then dumped.

Solver presents a constructor that receives its matrix argument and saves its reference in field data along with the number of rows in field N. The constructor then creates a cyclic barrier with N parties and a barrier action that's responsible for merging all of the rows into a final matrix. Finally, the constructor creates a worker thread that executes a separate Worker runnable that's responsible for processing a single row in the matrix. The constructor then waits until the workers are finished.

Worker's run() method repeatedly invokes processRow() on its specific row until done() returns true, which (in this example) it does after processRow() executes one time. After processRow() returns, which indicates that the row has been processed, the worker thread invokes await() on the cyclic barrier; it cannot proceed.

At some point, all of the worker threads will have invoked await(). When the final thread, which processes the final row in the matrix, invokes await(), it will trigger the barrier action, which merges all processed rows into a final matrix. In this example, a merger isn't required, but it would be required in more complex examples.

The final task performed by mergeRows() is to notify the main thread that invoked Solver's constructor. This thread is waiting on the monitor associated with String object "abc". A call to notify() suffices to wake up the waiting thread, which is the only thread waiting on this monitor.

Compile Listing 6-2 as follows:

```
javac CyclicBarrierDemo.java
```

Run the resulting application as follows:

```
java CyclicBarrierDemo
```

You should observe output that's similar to the following (message order may differ somewhat):

```
0.0 1.0 2.0
3.0 4.0 5.0
6.0 7.0 8.0

main thread waiting
Processing row: 0
Processing row: 1
Processing row: 2
merging
main thread notified

0.0 10.0 20.0
30.0 40.0 50.0
60.0 70.0 80.0
```

Exchangers

An *exchanger* provides a synchronization point where threads can swap objects. Each thread presents some object on entry to the exchanger's exchange() method, matches with a partner thread, and receives its partner's object on return. Exchangers can be useful in applications such as genetic algorithms (see http://en.wikipedia.org/wiki/Genetic_algorithm) and pipeline designs.

The generic `java.util.concurrent.Exchanger<V>` class implements the exchanger synchronizer. You initialize an exchanger by invoking the `Exchanger()` constructor. You then invoke either of the following methods to perform an exchange:

- `V exchange(V x)`: Wait for another thread to arrive at this exchange point (unless the calling thread is interrupted), and then transfer the given object to it, receiving the other thread's object in return. If another thread is already waiting at the exchange point, it's resumed for thread-scheduling purposes and receives the object passed in by the calling thread. The current thread returns immediately, receiving the object passed to the exchanger by the other thread. This method throws `InterruptedException` when the calling thread is interrupted.

- `V exchange(V x, long timeout, TimeUnit unit)`: This method is equivalent to the previous method except that it lets you specify how long the calling thread is willing to wait. It throws `TimeoutException` when this timeout expires while the thread is waiting.

Listing 6-3 expands on the repeated buffer filling and emptying `Exchanger` example presented in `Exchanger`'s Javadoc.

Listing 6-3. Using an Exchanger to Swap Buffers

```java
import java.util.ArrayList;
import java.util.List;

import java.util.concurrent.Exchanger;

public class ExchangerDemo
{
   final static Exchanger<DataBuffer> exchanger =
      new Exchanger<DataBuffer>();

   final static DataBuffer initialEmptyBuffer = new DataBuffer();
   final static DataBuffer initialFullBuffer = new DataBuffer("I");

   public static void main(String[] args)
   {
      class FillingLoop implements Runnable
      {
         int count = 0;

         @Override
         public void run()
         {
            DataBuffer currentBuffer = initialEmptyBuffer;
            try
```

```
      {
         while (true)
         {
            addToBuffer(currentBuffer);
            if (currentBuffer.isFull())
            {
               System.out.println("filling thread wants to exchange");
               currentBuffer = exchanger.exchange(currentBuffer);
               System.out.println("filling thread receives exchange");
            }
         }
      }
      catch (InterruptedException ie)
      {
         System.out.println("filling thread interrupted");
      }
   }

   void addToBuffer(DataBuffer buffer)
   {
      String item = "NI" + count++;
      System.out.println("Adding: " + item);
      buffer.add(item);
   }
}

class EmptyingLoop implements Runnable
{
   @Override
   public void run()
   {
      DataBuffer currentBuffer = initialFullBuffer;
      try
      {
         while (true)
         {
            takeFromBuffer(currentBuffer);
            if (currentBuffer.isEmpty())
            {
               System.out.println("emptying thread wants to " +
                                  "exchange");
               currentBuffer = exchanger.exchange(currentBuffer);
               System.out.println("emptying thread receives " +
                                  "exchange");
            }
         }
      }
```

```java
                    catch (InterruptedException ie)
                    {
                        System.out.println("emptying thread interrupted");
                    }
                }
                void takeFromBuffer(DataBuffer buffer)
                {
                    System.out.println("taking: " + buffer.remove());
                }
            }
        new Thread(new EmptyingLoop()).start();
        new Thread(new FillingLoop()).start();
    }
}

class DataBuffer
{
    private final static int MAXITEMS = 10;

    private final List<String> items = new ArrayList<>();

    DataBuffer()
    {
    }

    DataBuffer(String prefix)
    {
        for (int i = 0; i < MAXITEMS; i++)
        {
            String item = prefix + i;
            System.out.printf("Adding %s%n", item);
            items.add(item);
        }
    }

    synchronized void add(String s)
    {
        if (!isFull())
            items.add(s);
    }

    synchronized boolean isEmpty()
    {
        return items.size() == 0;
    }
```

```
   synchronized boolean isFull()
   {
      return items.size() == MAXITEMS;
   }

   synchronized String remove()
   {
      if (!isEmpty())
         return items.remove(0);
      return null;
   }
}
```

Listing 6-3's default main thread creates an exchanger and a pair of buffers via static field initializers. It then instantiates the EmptyingLoop and FillingLoop local classes and passes these runnables to new Thread instances whose threads are then started. (I could have used executors.) Each runnable's run() method enters an infinite loop that repeatedly adds to or removes from its buffer. When the buffer is full or empty, the exchanger is used to swap these buffers and the filling or emptying continues.

Compile Listing 6-3 as follows:

```
javac ExchangerDemo.java
```

Run the resulting application as follows:

```
java ExchangerDemo
```

You should observe a prefix of the output that's similar to the following (the message order may differ somewhat):

```
Adding I0
Adding I1
Adding I2
Adding I3
Adding I4
Adding I5
Adding I6
Adding I7
Adding I8
Adding I9
taking: I0
taking: I1
taking: I2
taking: I3
taking: I4
taking: I5
taking: I6
taking: I7
```

```
taking: I8
taking: I9
emptying thread wants to exchange
Adding: NI0
Adding: NI1
Adding: NI2
Adding: NI3
Adding: NI4
Adding: NI5
Adding: NI6
Adding: NI7
Adding: NI8
Adding: NI9
filling thread wants to exchange
filling thread receives exchange
emptying thread receives exchange
Adding: NI10
taking: NI0
Adding: NI11
taking: NI1
Adding: NI12
```

Semaphores

A *semaphore* maintains a set of *permits* for restricting the number of threads that can access a limited resource. A thread attempting to acquire a permit when no permits are available blocks until some other thread releases a permit.

■ **Note**   Semaphores whose current values can be incremented past 1 are known as *counting semaphores*, whereas semaphores whose current values can be only 0 or 1 are known as *binary semaphores* or *mutexes*. In either case, the current value cannot be negative.

The java.util.concurrent.Semaphore class implements this synchronizer and conceptualizes a semaphore as an object maintaining a set of *permits*. You initialize a semaphore by invoking the Semaphore(int permits) constructor where permits specifies the number of available permits. The resulting semaphore's *fairness policy* is set to false (unfair). Alternatively, you can invoke the Semaphore(int permits, boolean fair) constructor to also set the semaphore's fairness setting to true (fair).

SEMAPHORES AND FAIRNESS

When the fairness setting is `false`, Semaphore makes no guarantees about the order in which threads acquire permits. In particular, *barging* is permitted; that is, a thread invoking `acquire()` can be allocated a permit ahead of a thread that has been waiting—logically the new thread places itself at the head of the queue of waiting threads. When `fair` is set to `true`, the semaphore guarantees that threads invoking any of the `acquire()` methods are selected to obtain permits in the order in which their invocation of those methods was processed (first-in-first-out; FIFO). Because FIFO ordering necessarily applies to specific internal points of execution within these methods, it's possible for one thread to invoke `acquire()` before another thread but reach the ordering point after the other thread, and similarly upon return from the method. Also, the untimed `tryAcquire()` methods don't honor the fairness setting; they'll take any available permits.

Generally, semaphores used to control resource access should be initialized as fair, to ensure that no thread is starved out from accessing a resource. When using semaphores for other kinds of synchronization control, the throughput advantages of unfair ordering often outweigh fairness considerations.

Semaphore also offers the following methods:

- `void acquire()`: Acquire a permit from this semaphore, blocking until one is available or the calling thread is interrupted. `InterruptedException` is thrown when it's interrupted.

- `void acquire(int permits)`: Acquire `permits` permits from this semaphore, blocking until they are available or the calling thread is interrupted. `InterruptedException` is thrown when interrupted; `IllegalArgumentException` is thrown when `permits` is less than zero.

- `void acquireUninterruptibly()`: Acquire a permit, blocking until one is available.

- `void acquireUninterruptibly(int permits)`: Acquire `permits` permits, blocking until they are all available. `IllegalArgumentException` is thrown when `permits` is less than zero.

- `int availablePermits()`: Return the current number of available permits. This method is useful for debugging and testing.

- `int drainPermits()`: Acquire and return a count of all permits that are immediately available.

- `int getQueueLength()`: Return an estimate of the number of threads waiting to acquire permits. The returned value is only an estimate because the number of threads may change dynamically while this method traverses internal data structures. This method is designed for use in monitoring the system state and not for synchronization control.

- `boolean hasQueuedThreads()`: Query whether any threads are waiting to acquire permits. Because cancellations may occur at any time, a `true` return value doesn't guarantee that another thread will ever acquire permits. This method is designed mainly for use in monitoring the system state. It returns `true` when there may be other waiting threads.

- `boolean isFair()`: Return the fairness setting (`true` for fair and `false` for unfair).

- `void release()`: Release a permit, returning it to the semaphore. The number of available permits is increased by one. If any threads are trying to acquire a permit, one thread is selected and given the permit that was just released. That thread is reenabled for thread scheduling purposes.

- `void release(int permits)`: Release `permits` permits, returning them to the semaphore. The number of available permits is increased by `permits`. If any threads are trying to acquire permits, one is selected and given the permits that were just released. If the number of available permits satisfies that thread's request, the thread is reenabled for thread scheduling purposes; otherwise, the thread will wait until sufficient permits are available. If there are permits available after this thread's request has been satisfied, those permits are assigned to other threads trying to acquire permits. `IllegalArgumentException` is thrown when `permits` is less than zero.

- `String toString()`: Return a string identifying this semaphore as well as its state. The state, in brackets, includes the string literal `"Permits ="` followed by the number of permits.

- `boolean tryAcquire()`: Acquire a permit from this semaphore but only when one is available at the time of invocation. Return `true` when the permit was acquired. Otherwise, return immediately with value `false`.

- `boolean tryAcquire(int permits)`: Acquire `permits` permits from this semaphore but only when they are available at the time of invocation. Return `true` when the permits were acquired. Otherwise, return immediately with value `false`. `IllegalArgumentException` is thrown when `permits` is less than zero.

- `boolean tryAcquire(int permits, long timeout, TimeUnit unit)`: Like the previous method but the calling thread waits when `permits` permits aren't available. The wait ends when the permits become available, the timeout expires, or the calling thread is interrupted, in which case `InterruptedException` is thrown.

- `boolean tryAcquire(long timeOut, TimeUnit unit)`: Like `tryAcquire(int permits)` but the calling thread waits until a permit is available. The wait ends when the permit becomes available, the timeout expires, or the calling thread is interrupted, in which case `InterruptedException` is thrown.

Listing 6-4 expands on the "controlling access to a pool of items" Semaphore example presented in Semaphore's Javadoc.

Listing 6-4. Using a Counting Semaphore to Control Access to a Pool of Items

```java
import java.util.concurrent.Executors;
import java.util.concurrent.ExecutorService;
import java.util.concurrent.Semaphore;

public class SemaphoreDemo
{
   public static void main(String[] args)
   {
      final Pool pool = new Pool();
      Runnable r = new Runnable()
                   {
                      @Override
                      public void run()
                      {
                         String name = Thread.currentThread().getName();
                         try
                         {
                            while (true)
                            {
                               String item;
                               System.out.println(name + " acquiring " +
                                                  (item = pool.getItem()));
                               Thread.sleep(200 +
                                            (int) (Math.random() * 100));
                               System.out.println(name + " putting back " +
                                                  item);
                               pool.putItem(item);
                            }
                         }
                      }
```

```
                        catch (InterruptedException ie)
                        {
                            System.out.println(name + "interrupted");
                        }
                    }
                };
        ExecutorService[] executors =
            new ExecutorService[Pool.MAX_AVAILABLE + 1];
        for (int i = 0; i < executors.length; i++)
        {
            executors[i] = Executors.newSingleThreadExecutor();
            executors[i].execute(r);
        }
    }
}

final class Pool
{
    public static final int MAX_AVAILABLE = 10;

    private final Semaphore available = new Semaphore(MAX_AVAILABLE, true);

    private final String[] items;

    private final boolean[] used = new boolean[MAX_AVAILABLE];

    Pool()
    {
        items = new String[MAX_AVAILABLE];
        for (int i = 0; i < items.length; i++)
            items[i] = "I" + i;
    }

    String getItem() throws InterruptedException
    {
        available.acquire();
        return getNextAvailableItem();
    }

    void putItem(String item)
    {
        if (markAsUnused(item))
            available.release();
    }
```

```
private synchronized String getNextAvailableItem()
{
   for (int i = 0; i < MAX_AVAILABLE; ++i)
   {
      if (!used[i])
      {
         used[i] = true;
         return items[i];
      }
   }
   return null; // not reached
}

private synchronized boolean markAsUnused(String item)
{
   for (int i = 0; i < MAX_AVAILABLE; ++i)
   {
      if (item == items[i])
      {
         if (used[i])
         {
            used[i] = false;
            return true;
         }
         else
            return false;
      }
   }
   return false;
}
}
```

Listing 6-4's default main thread creates a resource pool, a runnable for repeatedly acquiring and putting back resources, and an array of executors. Each executor is told to execute the runnable.

Pool's String getItem() and void putItem(String item) methods obtain and return string-based resources. Before obtaining an item in getItem(), the calling thread must acquire a permit from the semaphore, which guarantees that an item is available for use. When the thread finishes with the item, it calls putItem(String), which returns the item to the pool and then releases a permit to the semaphore, which lets another thread acquire that item.

No synchronization lock is held when acquire() is called because that would prevent an item from being returned to the pool. However, String getNextAvailableItem() and boolean markAsUnused(String item) are synchronized to maintain pool consistency. (The semaphore encapsulates the synchronization for restricting access to the pool separately from the synchronization that's required for maintaining pool consistency.)

Compile Listing 6-4 as follows:

```
javac SemaphoreDemo.java
```

Run the resulting application as follows:

```
java SemaphoreDemo
```

You should observe a prefix of the output that's similar to the following (message order may differ somewhat):

```
pool-1-thread-1 acquiring I0
pool-2-thread-1 acquiring I1
pool-3-thread-1 acquiring I2
pool-5-thread-1 acquiring I3
pool-7-thread-1 acquiring I4
pool-4-thread-1 acquiring I5
pool-6-thread-1 acquiring I6
pool-9-thread-1 acquiring I7
pool-8-thread-1 acquiring I8
pool-10-thread-1 acquiring I9
pool-9-thread-1 putting back I7
pool-2-thread-1 putting back I1
pool-11-thread-1 acquiring I7
pool-9-thread-1 acquiring I1
pool-8-thread-1 putting back I8
pool-2-thread-1 acquiring I8
pool-5-thread-1 putting back I3
pool-8-thread-1 acquiring I3
pool-4-thread-1 putting back I5
pool-5-thread-1 acquiring I5
pool-6-thread-1 putting back I6
pool-4-thread-1 acquiring I6
pool-1-thread-1 putting back I0
pool-6-thread-1 acquiring I0
pool-7-thread-1 putting back I4
pool-1-thread-1 acquiring I4
pool-10-thread-1 putting back I9
pool-7-thread-1 acquiring I9
pool-3-thread-1 putting back I2
pool-10-thread-1 acquiring I2
```

Phasers

A *phaser* is a more flexible cyclic barrier. Like a cyclic barrier, a phaser lets a group of threads wait on a barrier; these threads continue after the last thread arrives. A phaser also offers the equivalent of a barrier action. Unlike a cyclic barrier, which coordinates a fixed number of threads, a phaser can coordinate a variable number of threads, which can register at any time. To implement this capability, a phaser uses phases and phase numbers.

A *phase* is the phaser's current state, and this state is identified by an integer-based *phase number*. When the last of the registered threads arrives at the phaser barrier, a phaser advances to the next phase and increments its phase number by 1.

The `java.util.concurrent.Phaser` class implements a phaser. Because this class is thoroughly described in its Javadoc, I'll point out only a few constructor and methods:

- The `Phaser(int threads)` constructor creates a phaser that initially coordinates nthreads threads (which have yet to arrive at the phaser barrier) and whose phase number is initially set to 0.

- The `int register()` method adds a new unarrived thread to this phaser and returns the phase number to classify the arrival. This number is known as the *arrival phase number*.

- The `int arriveAndAwaitAdvance()` method records arrival and waits for the phaser to advance (which happens after the other threads have arrived). It returns the phase number to which the arrival applies.

- The `int arriveAndDeregister()` method arrives at this phaser and deregisters from it without waiting for others to arrive, reducing the number of threads required to advance in future phases.

Listing 6-5 provides a demonstration of the phaser synchronizer. It's based on the first example in `Phaser`'s Javadoc.

Listing 6-5. Using a Phaser to Control a One-Shot Action Serving a Variable Number of Parties

```
import java.util.ArrayList;
import java.util.List;

import java.util.concurrent.Executors;
import java.util.concurrent.Phaser;

public class PhaserDemo
{
    public static void main(String[] args)
    {
        List<Runnable> tasks = new ArrayList<>();
        tasks.add(() -> System.out.printf("%s running at %d%n",
                                Thread.currentThread().getName(),
                                System.currentTimeMillis()));
```

```java
        tasks.add(() -> System.out.printf("%s running at %d%n",
                                          Thread.currentThread().getName(),
                                          System.currentTimeMillis()));
        runTasks(tasks);
    }

    static void runTasks(List<Runnable> tasks)
    {
        final Phaser phaser = new Phaser(1); // "1" (register self)
        // create and start threads
        for (final Runnable task: tasks)
        {
            phaser.register();
            Runnable r = () ->
                        {
                            try
                            {
                                Thread.sleep(50 + (int) (Math.random() * 300));
                            }
                            catch (InterruptedException ie)
                            {
                                System.out.println("interrupted thread");
                            }
                            phaser.arriveAndAwaitAdvance(); // await the ...
                                                            // creation of ...
                                                            // all tasks
                            task.run();
                        };
            Executors.newSingleThreadExecutor().execute(r);
        }
        // allow threads to start and deregister self
        phaser.arriveAndDeregister();
    }
}
```

Listing 6-5's default main thread creates a pair of runnable tasks that each report the time (in milliseconds) at which its starts to run. It then runs these tasks after creating a Phaser instance and waiting for both tasks to arrive at the barrier.

Compile Listing 6-5 as follows:

```
javac PhaserDemo.java
```

Run the resulting application as follows:

```
java PhaserDemo
```

You should observe output that's similar to the following (and the application should not end—press Ctrl+C or your keystroke equivalent to end the application):

```
pool-1-thread-1 running at 1445806012709
pool-2-thread-1 running at 1445806012712
```

As you would expect from countdown latch behavior, both threads start running at (in this case) the same time even though a thread may have been delayed by as much as 349 milliseconds thanks to the presence of Thread.sleep().

Comment out phaser.arriveAndAwaitAdvance(); // await the ... and you should now observe the threads starting at radically different times, as illustrated here:

```
pool-2-thread-1 running at 1445806212870
pool-1-thread-1 running at 1445806213013
```

EXERCISES

The following exercises are designed to test your understanding of Chapter 6's content:

1. Define synchronizer.

2. Describe the behavior of a countdown latch.

3. What happens when CountDownLatch's void countDown() method is called and the count reaches zero?

4. Describe the behavior of a cyclic barrier.

5. True or false: CyclicBarrier's int await() method returns -1 when the barrier is reset while any thread is waiting or when the barrier is broken when await() is invoked.

6. Describe the behavior of an exchanger.

7. What does Exchanger's V exchange(V x) method accomplish?

8. Describe the behavior of a semaphore.

9. Identify the two kinds of semaphores.

10. Describe the behavior of a phaser.

11. What does Phaser's int register() method return?

12. Listing 3-2 (in Chapter 3) presented an enhanced PC application. Recreate this application where the synchronization is handled by the Semaphore class.

Summary

Java provides the synchronized keyword for synchronizing thread access to critical sections. Because it can be difficult to correctly write synchronized code that's based on synchronized, high-level synchronizers are included in the concurrency utilities.

A countdown latch causes one or more threads to wait at a "gate" until another thread opens this gate, at which point these other threads can continue. It consists of a count and operations for "causing a thread to wait until the count reaches zero" and "decrementing the count."

A cyclic barrier lets a set of threads wait for each other to reach a common barrier point. The barrier is cyclic because it can be reused after the waiting threads are released. This synchronizer is useful in applications involving a fixed-size party of threads that must occasionally wait for each other.

An exchanger provides a synchronization point where threads can swap objects. Each thread presents some object on entry to the exchanger's exchange() method, matches with a partner thread, and receives its partner's object on return.

A semaphore maintains a set of permits for restricting the number of threads that can access a limited resource. A thread attempting to acquire a permit when no permits are available blocks until some other thread releases a permit.

A phaser is a more flexible cyclic barrier. Like a cyclic barrier, a phaser lets a group of threads wait on a barrier; these threads continue after the last thread arrives. A phaser also offers the equivalent of a barrier action. Unlike a cyclic barrier, which coordinates a fixed number of threads, a phaser can coordinate a variable number of threads, which can register at any time. To implement this capability, a phaser uses phases and phase numbers.

Chapter 7 presents the Locking Framework.

CHAPTER 7

■ ■ ■

The Locking Framework

The java.util.concurrent.locks package provides a framework of interfaces and classes for locking and waiting for conditions in a manner that's distinct from an object's intrinsic lock-based synchronization and java.lang.Object's wait/notification mechanism. The concurrency utilities include the Locking Framework that improves on intrinsic synchronization and wait/notification by offering lock polling, timed waits, and more.

SYNCHRONIZED AND LOW-LEVEL LOCKING

Java supports synchronization so that threads can safely update shared variables and ensure that a thread's updates are visible to other threads. You leverage synchronization in your code by marking methods or code blocks with the synchronized keyword. These code sequences are known as *critical sections*. The Java virtual machine (JVM) supports synchronization via monitors and the monitorenter and monitorexit JVM instructions.

Every Java object is associated with a *monitor*, which is a *mutual exclusion* (letting only one thread at a time execute in a critical section) construct that prevents multiple threads from concurrently executing in a critical section. Before a thread can enter a critical section, it's required to lock the monitor. If the monitor is already locked, the thread blocks until the monitor is unlocked (by another thread leaving the critical section).

When a thread locks a monitor in a multicore/multiprocessor environment, the values of shared variables that are stored in main memory are read into the copies of these variables that are stored in a thread's *working memory* (also known as *local memory* or *cache memory*). This action ensures that the thread will work with the most recent values of these variables and not stale values, and is known as *visibility*. The thread proceeds to work with its copies of these shared variables. When the thread unlocks the monitor while leaving the critical section, the values in its copies of shared variables are written back to main memory, which lets the next thread that enters the critical section access the most recent values of these variables. (The volatile keyword addresses visibility only.)

The Locking Framework includes the often-used Lock, ReentrantLock, Condition, ReadWriteLock, and ReentrantReadWriteLock types, which I explore in this chapter. I also briefly introduce you to the StampedLock class, which was introduced by Java 8.

Lock

The Lock interface offers more extensive locking operations than can be obtained via the locks associated with monitors. For example, you can immediately back out of a lock-acquisition attempt when a lock isn't available. This interface declares the following methods:

- void lock(): Acquire the lock. When the lock isn't available, the calling thread is forced to wait until it becomes available.

- void lockInterruptibly(): Acquire the lock unless the calling thread is interrupted. When the lock isn't available, the calling thread is forced to wait until it becomes available or the thread is interrupted, which results in this method throwing java.lang. InterruptedException.

- Condition newCondition(): Return a new Condition instance that's bound to this Lock instance. This method throws java.lang.UnsupportedOperationException when the Lock implementation class doesn't support conditions.

- boolean tryLock(): Acquire the lock when it's available at the time this method is invoked. The method returns true when the lock is acquired and false when the lock isn't acquired.

- boolean tryLock(long time, TimeUnit unit): Acquire the lock when it's available within the specified waiting time, measured in unit java.util.concurrent.TimeUnit units (seconds, milliseconds, and so on), and the calling thread isn't interrupted. When the lock isn't available, the calling thread is forced to wait until it becomes available within the waiting time or the thread is interrupted, which results in this method throwing InterruptedException. When the lock is acquired, true is returned; otherwise, false returns.

- void unlock(): Release the lock.

Acquired locks must be released. In the context of synchronized methods and blocks and the implicit monitor lock associated with every object, all lock acquisition and release occurs in a block-structured manner. When multiple locks are acquired, they're released in the opposite order and all locks are released in the same lexical scope in which they were acquired.

Lock acquisition and release in the context of Lock interface implementations can be more flexible. For example, some algorithms for traversing concurrently accessed data structures require the use of "hand-over-hand" or "chain locking": you acquire the lock of node A, then node B, then release A and acquire C, then release B and acquire D, and so on. Implementations of the Lock interface enable the use of such techniques by allowing a lock to be acquired and released in different scopes, and by allowing multiple locks to be acquired and released in any order.

With this increased flexibility comes additional responsibility. The absence of block-structured locking removes the automatic release of locks that occurs with synchronized methods and blocks. As a result, you should typically employ the following idiom for lock acquisition and release:

```
Lock l = ...; // ... is a placeholder for code that obtains the lock
l.lock();
try
{
  // access the resource protected by this lock
}
catch (Exception ex)
{
  // restore invariants
}
finally
{
    l.unlock();
}
```

This idiom ensures that an acquired lock will always be released.

■ **Note**   All Lock implementations are required to enforce the same memory synchronization semantics as provided by the built-in monitor lock.

ReentrantLock

Lock is implemented by the ReentrantLock class, which describes a reentrant mutual exclusion lock. This lock is associated with a hold count. When a thread holds the lock and reacquires the lock by invoking lock(), lockUninterruptibly(), or one of the tryLock() methods, the hold count is increased by 1. When the thread invokes unlock(), the hold count is decremented by 1. The lock is released when this count reaches 0.

ReentrantLock offers the same concurrency and memory semantics as the implicit monitor lock that's accessed via synchronized methods and blocks. However, it has extended capabilities and offers better performance under high *thread contention* (threads frequently asking to acquire a lock that's already held by another thread). When many threads attempt to access a shared resource, the JVM spends less time scheduling these threads and more time executing them.

You initialize a ReentrantLock instance by invoking either of the following constructors:

- ReentrantLock(): Create an instance of ReentrantLock. This constructor is equivalent to ReentrantLock(false).

- ReentrantLock(boolean fair): Create an instance of ReentrantLock with the specified fairness policy. Pass true to fair when this lock should use a fair ordering policy: under contention, the lock would favor granting access to the longest-waiting thread.

ReentrantLock implements Lock's methods. However, its implementation of unlock() throws java.lang.IllegalMonitorStateException when the calling thread doesn't hold the lock. Also, ReentrantLock provides its own methods. For example, boolean isFair() returns the fairness policy and boolean isHeldByCurrentThread() returns true when the lock is held by the current thread. Listing 7-1 demonstrates ReentrantLock.

Listing 7-1. Achieving Synchronization in Terms of Reentrant Locks

```
import java.util.concurrent.Executors;
import java.util.concurrent.ExecutorService;
import java.util.concurrent.TimeUnit;

import java.util.concurrent.locks.ReentrantLock;

public class RLDemo
{
   public static void main(String[] args)
   {
      ExecutorService executor = Executors.newFixedThreadPool(2);
      final ReentrantLock lock = new ReentrantLock();

      class Worker implements Runnable
      {
         private final String name;

         Worker(String name)
         {
            this.name = name;
         }

         @Override
         public void run()
         {
            lock.lock();
            try
```

```
      {
          if (lock.isHeldByCurrentThread())
             System.out.printf("Thread %s entered critical section.%n",name);
          System.out.printf("Thread %s performing work.%n", name);
          try
          {
             Thread.sleep(2000);
          }
          catch (InterruptedException ie)
          {
             ie.printStackTrace();
          }
          System.out.printf("Thread %s finished working.%n", name);
      }
      finally
      {
          lock.unlock();
      }
   }
}
executor.execute(new Worker("ThdA"));
executor.execute(new Worker("ThdB"));
try
{
   executor.awaitTermination(5, TimeUnit.SECONDS);
}
catch (InterruptedException ie)
{
   ie.printStackTrace();
}
executor.shutdownNow();
   }
}
```

Listing 7-1 describes an application whose default main thread creates a pair of worker threads that enter, simulate working in, and leave critical sections. They use ReentrantLock's lock() and unlock() methods to obtain and release a reentrant lock. When a thread calls lock() and the lock is unavailable, the thread is disabled (and cannot be scheduled) until the lock becomes available.

Compile Listing 7-1 as follows:

```
javac RLDemo.java
```

Run the resulting application as follows:

```
java RLDemo
```

You should discover output that's similar to the following (message order may differ somewhat):

```
Thread ThdA entered critical section.
Thread ThdA performing work.
Thread ThdA finished working.
Thread ThdB entered critical section.
Thread ThdB performing work.
Thread ThdB finished working.
```

Condition

The Condition interface factors out Object's wait and notification methods (wait(), notify(), and notifyAll()) into distinct condition objects to give the effect of having multiple wait-sets per object, by combining them with the use of arbitrary Lock implementations. Where Lock replaces synchronized methods and blocks, Condition replaces Object's wait/notification methods.

■ **Note**   A Condition instance is intrinsically bound to a lock. To obtain a Condition instance for a certain Lock instance, use Lock's newCondition() method.

Condition declares the following methods:

- void await(): Force the calling thread to wait until it's signaled or interrupted.

- boolean await(long time, TimeUnit unit): Force the calling thread to wait until it's signaled or interrupted, or until the specified waiting time elapses.

- long awaitNanos(long nanosTimeout): Force the current thread to wait until it's signaled or interrupted, or until the specified waiting time elapses.

- void awaitUninterruptibly(): Force the current thread to wait until it's signaled.

- boolean awaitUntil(Date deadline): Force the current thread to wait until it's signaled or interrupted, or until the specified deadline elapses.

- void signal(): Wake up one waiting thread.

- void signalAll(): Wake up all waiting threads.

Listing 7-2 revisits Chapter 3's producer-consumer application (in Listing 3-2) to show you how it can be written to take advantage of conditions.

Listing 7-2. Achieving Synchronization in Terms of Locks and Conditions

```java
import java.util.concurrent.locks.Condition;
import java.util.concurrent.locks.Lock;
import java.util.concurrent.locks.ReentrantLock;

public class PC
{
   public static void main(String[] args)
   {
      Shared s = new Shared();
      new Producer(s).start();
      new Consumer(s).start();
   }
}

class Shared
{
   private char c;

   private volatile boolean available;

   private final Lock lock;

   private final Condition condition;

   Shared()
   {
      available = false;
      lock = new ReentrantLock();
      condition = lock.newCondition();
   }

   Lock getLock()
   {
      return lock;
   }

   char getSharedChar()
   {
      lock.lock();
      try
      {
         while (!available)
            try
            {
               condition.await();
            }
```

```java
                catch (InterruptedException ie)
                {
                    ie.printStackTrace();
                }
            available = false;
            condition.signal();
        }
        finally
        {
            lock.unlock();
            return c;
        }
    }

    void setSharedChar(char c)
    {
        lock.lock();
        try
        {
            while (available)
                try
                {
                    condition.await();
                }
                catch (InterruptedException ie)
                {
                    ie.printStackTrace();
                }
            this.c = c;
            available = true;
            condition.signal();
        }
        finally
        {
            lock.unlock();
        }
    }
}
class Producer extends Thread
{
    private final Lock l;

    private final Shared s;
```

```
   Producer(Shared s)
   {
      this.s = s;
      l = s.getLock();
   }

   @Override
   public void run()
   {
      for (char ch = 'A'; ch <= 'Z'; ch++)
      {
         l.lock();
         s.setSharedChar(ch);
         System.out.println(ch + " produced by producer.");
         l.unlock();
      }
   }
}

class Consumer extends Thread
{
   private final Lock l;

   private final Shared s;

   Consumer(Shared s)
   {
      this.s = s;
      l = s.getLock();
   }

   @Override
   public void run()
   {
      char ch;
      do
      {
         l.lock();
         ch = s.getSharedChar();
         System.out.println(ch + " consumed by consumer.");
         l.unlock();
      }
      while (ch != 'Z');
   }
}
```

Listing 7-2 is similar to Listing 3-2's PC application. However, it replaces synchronized and wait/notification with locks and conditions.

PC's main() method instantiates the Shared, Producer, and Consumer classes. The Shared instance is passed to the Producer and Consumer constructors and these threads are then started.

The Producer and Consumer constructors are called on the default main thread. Because the Shared instance is also accessed by the producer and consumer threads, this instance must be visible to these threads (especially when these threads run on different cores). In each of Producer and Consumer, I accomplish this task by declaring s to be final. I could have declared this field to be volatile, but volatile suggests additional writes to the field and s shouldn't be changed after being initialized.

Check out Shared's constructor. Notice that it creates a lock via lock = new ReentrantLock();, and creates a condition associated with this lock via condition = lock.newCondition();. This lock is made available to the producer and consumer threads via the Lock getLock() method.

The producer thread invokes Shared's void setSharedChar(char c) method to generate a new character and then outputs a message identifying the produced character. This method locks the previously created Lock object and enters a while loop that repeatedly tests variable available, which is true when a produced character is available for consumption.

While available is true, the producer invokes the condition's await() method to wait for available to become false. The consumer signals the condition to wake up the producer when it has consumed the character. (I use a loop instead of an if statement because spurious wakeups are possible and available might still be true.)

After leaving its loop, the producer thread records the new character, assigns true to available to indicate that a new character is available for consumption, and signals the condition to wake up a waiting consumer. Lastly, it unlocks the lock and exits setSharedChar().

■ **Note** I lock the setSharedChar()/System.out.println() block in Producer's run() method and the getSharedChar()/System.out.println() block in Consumer's run() method to prevent the application from outputting consuming messages before producing messages, even though characters are produced before they're consumed.

The behavior of the consumer thread and getSharedChar() method is similar to what I've just described for the producer thread and setSharedChar() method.

■ **Note** I didn't use the try/finally idiom for ensuring that a lock is disposed of in Producer's and Consumer's run() methods because an exception isn't thrown from this context.

Compile Listing 7-2 as follows:

```
javac PC.java
```

Run the resulting application as follows:

```
java PC
```

You should observe output that's identical to the following prefix of the output, which indicates *lockstep synchronization* (the producer thread doesn't produce an item until it's consumed and the consumer thread doesn't consume an item until it's produced):

```
A produced by producer.
A consumed by consumer.
B produced by producer.
B consumed by consumer.
C produced by producer.
C consumed by consumer.
D produced by producer.
D consumed by consumer.
```

ReadWriteLock

Situations arise where data structures are read more often than they're modified. For example, you might have created an online dictionary of word definitions that many threads will read concurrently, while a single thread might occasionally add new definitions or update existing definitions. The Locking Framework provides a read-write locking mechanism for these situations that yields greater concurrency when reading and the safety of exclusive access when writing. This mechanism is based on the ReadWriteLock interface.

ReadWriteLock maintains a pair of locks: one lock for read-only operations and one lock for write operations. The read lock may be held simultaneously by multiple reader threads as long as there are no writers. The write lock is exclusive: only a single thread can modify shared data. (The lock that's associated with the synchronized keyword is also exclusive.)

ReadWriteLock declares the following methods:

- Lock readLock(): Return the lock that's used for reading.

- Lock writeLock(): Return the lock that's used for writing.

ReentrantReadWriteLock

ReadWriteLock is implemented by the ReentrantReadWriteLock class, which describes a reentrant read-write lock with similar semantics to ReentrantLock.

You initialize a ReentrantReadWriteLock instance by invoking either of the following constructors:

- ReentrantReadWriteLock(): Create an instance of ReentrantReadWriteLock. This constructor is equivalent to ReentrantReadWriteLock(false).

- ReentrantReadWriteLock(boolean fair): Create an instance of ReentrantReadWriteLock with the specified fairness policy. Pass true to fair when this lock should use a fair ordering policy.

■ **Note**   For the fair ordering policy, when the currently held lock is released, either the longest-waiting single writer thread will be assigned the write lock or, when there's a group of reader threads waiting longer than all waiting writer threads, that group will be assigned the read lock.

A thread that tries to acquire a fair read lock (non-reentrantly) will block when the write lock is held or when there's a waiting writer thread. The thread will not acquire the read lock until after the oldest currently waiting writer thread has acquired and released the write lock. If a waiting writer abandons its wait, leaving one or more reader threads as the longest waiters in the queue with the write lock free, those readers will be assigned the read lock.

A thread that tries to acquire a fair write lock (non-reentrantly) will block unless both the read lock and write lock are free (which implies no waiting threads). (The nonblocking tryLock() methods don't honor this fair setting and will immediately acquire the lock if possible, regardless of waiting threads.)

After instantiating this class, you invoke the following methods to obtain the read and write locks:

- ReentrantReadWriteLock.ReadLock readLock(): Return the lock used for reading.

- ReentrantReadWriteLock.WriteLock writeLock(): Return the lock used for writing.

Each of the nested ReadLock and WriteLock classes implements the Lock interface and declares its own methods. Furthermore, ReentrantReadWriteLock declares additional methods such as the following pair:

- int getReadHoldCount(): Return the number of reentrant read holds on this lock by the calling thread, which is 0 when the read lock isn't held by the calling thread. A reader thread has a hold on a lock for each lock action that's not matched by an unlock action.

- int getWriteHoldCount(): Return the number of reentrant write holds on this lock by the calling thread, which is 0 when the write lock isn't held by the calling thread. A writer thread has a hold on a lock for each lock action that's not matched by an unlock action.

To demonstrate ReadWriteLock and ReentrantReadWriteLock, Listing 7-3 presents an application whose writer thread populates a dictionary of word/definition entries while a reader thread continually accesses entries at random and outputs them.

Listing 7-3. Using ReadWriteLock to Satisfy a Dictionary Application's Reader and Writer Threads

```
import java.util.HashMap;
import java.util.Map;

import java.util.concurrent.Executors;
import java.util.concurrent.ExecutorService;

import java.util.concurrent.locks.Lock;
import java.util.concurrent.locks.ReadWriteLock;
import java.util.concurrent.locks.ReentrantReadWriteLock;

public class Dictionary
{
   public static void main(String[] args)
   {
      final String[] words =
      {
         "hypocalcemia",
         "prolixity",
         "assiduous",
         "indefatigable",
         "castellan"
      };

      final String[] definitions =
      {
         "a deficiency of calcium in the blood",
         "unduly prolonged or drawn out",
         "showing great care, attention, and effort",
```

```java
   "able to work or continue for a lengthy time without tiring",
   "the govenor or warden of a castle or fort"
};

final Map<String, String> dictionary = new HashMap<String, String>();

ReadWriteLock rwl = new ReentrantReadWriteLock(true);
final Lock rlock = rwl.readLock();
final Lock wlock = rwl.writeLock();

Runnable writer = () ->
                 {
                     for (int i = 0; i < words.length; i++)
                     {
                         wlock.lock();
                         try
                         {
                             dictionary.put(words[i],
                                             definitions[i]);
                             System.out.println("writer storing " +
                                                  words[i] + " entry");
                         }
                         finally
                         {
                             wlock.unlock();
                         }

                         try
                         {
                             Thread.sleep(1);
                         }
                         catch (InterruptedException ie)
                         {
                             System.err.println("writer " +
                                                  "interrupted");
                         }
                     }
                 };
   ExecutorService es = Executors.newFixedThreadPool(1);
   es.submit(writer);

   Runnable reader = () ->
                    {
                        while (true)
                        {
                            rlock.lock();
                            try
                            {
```

```
                    int i = (int) (Math.random() *
                                    words.length);
                    System.out.println("reader accessing " +
                                    words[i] + ": " +
                                    dictionary.get(words[i])
                                    + " entry");
               }
               finally
               {
                    rlock.unlock();
               }
          }
     };
   es = Executors.newFixedThreadPool(1);
   es.submit(reader);
 }
}
```

Listing 7-3's default main thread first creates the words and definitions arrays of strings, which are declared final because they will be accessed from anonymous classes. After creating a map in which to store word/definition entries, it obtains a reentrant read/write lock and accesses the reader and writer locks.

A runnable for the writer thread is now created. Its run() method iterates over the words array. Each of the iterations locks the writer lock. When this method returns, the writer thread has the exclusive writer lock and can update the map. It does so by invoking the map's put() method. After outputting a message to identify the added word, the writer thread releases the lock and sleeps one millisecond to give the appearance of performing other work. An executor based on a thread pool is obtained and used to invoke the writer thread's runnable.

A runnable for the reader thread is subsequently created. Its run() method repeatedly obtains the read lock, accesses a random entry in the map, outputs this entry, and unlocks the read lock. An executor based on a thread pool is obtained and used to invoke the reader thread's runnable.

Although I could have avoided the idiom for lock acquisition and release because an exception isn't thrown, I specified try/finally for good form.

Compile Listing 7-3 as follows:

```
javac Dictionary.java
```

Run the resulting application as follows:

```
java Dictionary
```

You should observe output that's similar to the following prefix of the output (the message order may differ somewhat) that I observed in one execution:

```
writer storing hypocalcemia entry
writer storing prolixity entry
reader accessing hypocalcemia: a deficiency of calcium in the blood entry
writer storing assiduous entry
reader accessing assiduous: showing great care, attention, and effort entry
reader accessing castellan: null entry
reader accessing hypocalcemia: a deficiency of calcium in the blood entry
reader accessing assiduous: showing great care, attention, and effort entry
reader accessing indefatigable: null entry
reader accessing hypocalcemia: a deficiency of calcium in the blood entry
reader accessing hypocalcemia: a deficiency of calcium in the blood entry
reader accessing assiduous: showing great care, attention, and effort entry
reader accessing indefatigable: null entry
reader accessing prolixity: unduly prolonged or drawn out entry
reader accessing hypocalcemia: a deficiency of calcium in the blood entry
reader accessing castellan: null entry
reader accessing assiduous: showing great care, attention, and effort entry
reader accessing hypocalcemia: a deficiency of calcium in the blood entry
reader accessing prolixity: unduly prolonged or drawn out entry
reader accessing assiduous: showing great care, attention, and effort entry
reader accessing castellan: null entry
reader accessing hypocalcemia: a deficiency of calcium in the blood entry
reader accessing indefatigable: null entry
reader accessing castellan: null entry
reader accessing prolixity: unduly prolonged or drawn out entry
reader accessing hypocalcemia: a deficiency of calcium in the blood entry
writer storing indefatigable entry
reader accessing assiduous: showing great care, attention, and effort entry
reader accessing assiduous: showing great care, attention, and effort entry
```

■ **Note**   Java 8 added StampedLock to the java.util.concurrent.locks package. According to its JDK 8 documentation, StampedLock is a capability-based lock with three modes for controlling read/write access. It differentiates between exclusive and nonexclusive locks in a manner that's similar to ReentrantReadWriteLock, but also allows for optimistic reads, which ReentrantReadWriteLock doesn't support. Check out Dr. Heinz Kabutz's *Phaser and StampedLock Concurrency Synchronizers* video presentation (www.parleys.com/tutorial/5148922b0364bc17fc56ca4f/chapter0/about) to learn about StampedLock. Also, see this presentation's PDF file (www.jfokus.se/jfokus13/preso/jf13_PhaserAndStampedLock.pdf).

EXERCISES

The following exercises are designed to test your understanding of Chapter 7's content:

1. Define lock.

2. What is the biggest advantage that Lock objects hold over the intrinsic locks that are obtained when threads enter critical sections (controlled via the synchronized reserved word)?

3. True or false: ReentrantLock's unlock() method throws IllegalMonitorStateException when the calling thread doesn't hold the lock.

4. How do you obtain a Condition instance for use with a particular Lock instance?

5. True or false: ReentrantReadWriteLock() creates an instance of ReentrantReadWriteLock with a fair ordering policy.

6. Define StampedLock.

7. The java.util.concurrent.locks package includes a LockSupport class. What is the purpose of LockSupport?

8. Replace the following ID class with an equivalent class that uses ReentrantLock in place of synchronized:

```
public class ID
{
    private static int counter; // initialized to 0 by default

    public static synchronized int getID()
    {
        int temp = counter + 1;
        try
        {
            Thread.sleep(1);
        }
        catch (InterruptedException ie)
        {
        }
        return counter = temp;
    }
}
```

Summary

The java.util.concurrent.locks package provides a framework of interfaces and classes for locking and waiting for conditions in a manner that's distinct from an object's intrinsic lock-based synchronization and Object's wait/notification mechanism. The concurrency utilities include a locking framework that improves on intrinsic synchronization and wait/notification by offering lock polling, timed waits, and more.

The Locking Framework includes the often-used Lock, ReentrantLock, Condition, ReadWriteLock, and ReentrantReadWriteLock types, which I explored in this chapter. I also briefly introduced you to the StampedLock class, which was introduced in Java 8.

Chapter 8 presents additional concurrency utilities.

CHAPTER 8

■ ■ ■

Additional Concurrency Utilities

Chapters 5 through 7 introduced you to the concurrency utilities, executors (and callables and futures), synchronizers, and the Locking Framework. In this chapter, I complete my coverage of the concurrency utilities by introducing you to concurrent collections, atomic variables, the Fork/Join Framework, and completion services.

■ **Note** Lack of time prevented my also covering completable futures. If you're interested in this topic, I recommend that you check out Tomasz Nurkiewicz's excellent blog post titled "Java 8: Definitive guide to CompletableFuture" at http://www.nurkiewicz.com/2013/05/java-8-definitive-guide-to.html.

Concurrent Collections

Java's Collections Framework provides interfaces and classes that are located in the java.util package. Interfaces include List, Set, and Map; classes include ArrayList, TreeSet, and HashMap.

ArrayList, TreeSet, HashMap, and other classes that implement these interfaces are not thread-safe. However, you can make them thread-safe by using the synchronized wrapper methods located in the java.util.Collections class. For example, you can pass an ArrayList instance to Collections.synchronizedList() to obtain a thread-safe variant of ArrayList.

Although they're often needed to simplify code in a multithreaded environment, there are a couple of problems with thread-safe collections:

- It's necessary to acquire a lock before iterating over a collection that might be modified by another thread during the iteration. If a lock isn't acquired and the collection is modified, it's highly likely that java.util.ConcurrentModificationException will be thrown. This happens because Collections Framework classes return *fail-fast iterators*, which are iterators that throw ConcurrentModificationException when collections are modified during iteration. Fail-fast iterators are often inconvenient to concurrent applications.

- Performance suffers when synchronized collections are accessed frequently from multiple threads. This performance problem ultimately impacts an application's *scalability*.

The concurrency utilities address these problems by including *concurrent collections*, which are concurrency performant and highly-scalable collections-oriented types that are stored in the java.util.concurrent package. Its collections-oriented classes return *weakly-consistent iterators*, which are iterators that have the following properties:

- An element that's removed after iteration starts but hasn't yet been returned via the iterator's next() method won't be returned.

- An element that's added after iteration starts may or may not be returned.

- No element is returned more than once during the iteration of a collection, regardless of changes made to the collection during iteration.

The following list offers a short sample of concurrency-oriented collection types that you'll find in the java.util.concurrent package:

- BlockingQueue is a subinterface of java.util.Queue that also supports blocking operations that wait for the queue to become nonempty before retrieving an element and wait for space to become available in the queue before storing an element. Each of the ArrayBlockingQueue, DelayQueue, LinkedBlockingQueue, PriorityBlockingQueue, and SynchronousQueue classes implements this interface directly. The LinkedBlockingDeque and LinkedTransferQueue classes implement this interface via BlockingQueue subinterfaces.

- ConcurrentMap is a subinterface of java.util.Map that declares additional indivisible putIfAbsent(), remove(), and replace() methods. The ConcurrentHashMap class (the concurrent equivalent of java.util.HashMap), the ConcurrentNavigableMap class, and the ConcurrentSkipListMap class implement this interface.

Oracle's Javadoc for BlockingQueue, ArrayBlockingQueue, and other concurrency-oriented collection types identifies these types as part of the Collections Framework.

Using BlockingQueue and ArrayBlockingQueue

BlockingQueue's Javadoc reveals the heart of a producer-consumer application that's vastly simpler than the equivalent application shown in Chapter 3 (see Listing 3-1) because it doesn't have to deal with synchronization. Listing 8-1 uses BlockingQueue and its ArrayBlockingQueue implementation class in a high-level producer-consumer equivalent.

Listing 8-1. The Blocking Queue Equivalent of Chapter 3's PC Application

```java
import java.util.concurrent.ArrayBlockingQueue;
import java.util.concurrent.BlockingQueue;
import java.util.concurrent.ExecutorService;
import java.util.concurrent.Executors;

public class PC
{
   public static void main(String[] args)
   {
      final BlockingQueue<Character> bq;
      bq = new ArrayBlockingQueue<Character>(26);
      final ExecutorService executor = Executors.newFixedThreadPool(2);
      Runnable producer = () ->
                          {
                             for (char ch = 'A'; ch <= 'Z'; ch++)
                             {
                                try
                                {
                                   bq.put(ch);
                                   System.out.printf("%c produced by " +
                                                "producer.%n", ch);
                                }
                                catch (InterruptedException ie)
                                {
                                }
                             }
                          };
```

```
        executor.execute(producer);
        Runnable consumer = () ->
                            {
                                char ch = '\0';
                                do
                                {
                                    try
                                    {
                                        ch = bq.take();
                                        System.out.printf("%c consumed by " +
                                                            "consumer.%n", ch);
                                    }
                                    catch (InterruptedException ie)
                                    {
                                    }
                                }
                                while (ch != 'Z');
                                executor.shutdownNow();
                            };
        executor.execute(consumer);
    }
}
```

Listing 8-1 uses BlockingQueue's put() and take() methods, respectively, to put an object on the blocking queue and to remove an object from the blocking queue. put() blocks when there's no room to put an object; take() blocks when the queue is empty.

Although BlockingQueue ensures that a character is never consumed before it's produced, this application's output may indicate otherwise. For example, here's a portion of the output from one run:

```
Y consumed by consumer.
Y produced by producer.
Z consumed by consumer.
Z produced by producer.
```

Chapter 3's PC application in Listing 3-2 overcame this incorrect output order by introducing an extra layer of synchronization around setSharedChar()/System.out. println() and an extra layer of synchronization around getSharedChar()/System.out. println(). Chapter 7's PC application in Listing 7-2 overcame this incorrect output order by placing these method calls between lock()/unlock() method calls.

Learning More About ConcurrentHashMap

The ConcurrentHashMap class behaves like HashMap but has been designed to work in multithreaded contexts without the need for explicit synchronization. For example, you often need to check if a map contains a specific value and, when this value is absent, put this value into the map:

```
if (!map.containsKey("some string-based key"))
   map.put("some string-based key", "some string-based value");
```

Although this code is simple and appears to do the job, it isn't thread-safe. Between the call to map.containsKey() and map.put(), another thread could insert this entry, which would then be overwritten. To fix this race condition, you must explicitly synchronize this code, which I demonstrate here:

```
synchronized(map)
{
   if (!map.containsKey("some string-based key"))
     map.put("some string-based key", "some string-based value");
}
```

The problem with this approach is that you've locked the entire map for read and write operations while checking for key existence and adding the entry to the map when the key doesn't exist. This locking affects performance when many threads are trying to access the map.

The generic ConcurrentHashMap<V> class addresses this problem by providing the V putIfAbsent(K key, V value) method, which introduces a key/value entry into the map when key is absent. This method is equivalent to the following code fragment but offers better performance:

```
synchronized(map)
{
   if (!map.containsKey(key))
     return map.put(key, value);
   else
     return map.get(key);
}
```

Using putIfAbsent(), the earlier code fragment translates into the following simpler code fragment:

```
map.putIfAbsent("some string-based key", "some string-based value");
```

■ **Note** Java 8 has improved ConcurrentHashMap by adding more than 30 new methods, which largely support lambda expressions and the Streams API via aggregate operations. Methods that perform aggregate operations include forEach() methods (forEach(), forEachKey(), forEachValue(), and forEachEntry()), search methods (search(), searchKeys(), searchValues(), and searchEntries()), and reduction methods (reduce(), reduceToDouble(), reduceToLong(), and so on). Miscellaneous methods (such as mappingCount() and newKeySet()) have been added as well. As a result of the JDK 8 changes, ConcurrentHashMaps (and classes built from them) are now more useful as caches. Cache-improvement changes include methods to compute values for keys, plus improved support for scanning (and possibly evicting) entries, as well as better support for maps with large numbers of elements.

Atomic Variables

The intrinsic locks that are associated with object monitors have historically suffered from poor performance. Although performance has improved, they still present a bottleneck when creating web servers and other applications that require high scalability and performance in the presence of significant thread contention.

A lot of research has gone into creating nonblocking algorithms that can radically improve performance in synchronization contexts. These algorithms offer increased scalability because threads don't block when multiple threads contend for the same data. Also, threads don't suffer from deadlock and other liveness problems.

Java 5 provided the ability to create efficient nonblocking algorithms by introducing the java.util.concurrent.atomic package. According to this package's JDK documentation, java.util.concurrent.atomic provides a small toolkit of classes that support lock-free, thread-safe operations on single variables.

The classes in the java.util.concurrent.atomic package extend the notion of volatile values, fields, and array elements to those that also provide an atomic conditional update so that external synchronization isn't required. In other words, you get mutual exclusion along with the memory semantics associated with volatile variables without external synchronization.

■ **Note** The terms *atomic* and *indivisible* are widely considered to be equivalent even though we can split the atom.

Some of the classes located in `java.util.concurrent.atomic` are described here:

- `AtomicBoolean`: A boolean value that may be updated atomically.

- `AtomicInteger`: An int value that may be updated atomically.

- `AtomicIntegerArray`: An int array whose elements may be updated atomically.

- `AtomicLong`: A long value that may be updated atomically.

- `AtomicLongArray`: A long array whose elements may be updated atomically.

- `AtomicReference`: An object reference that may be updated atomically.

- `AtomicReferenceArray`: An object reference array whose elements may be updated atomically.

Atomic variables are used to implement counters, sequence generators (such as `java.util.concurrent.ThreadLocalRandom`), and other constructs that require mutual exclusion without performance problems under high thread contention. For example, consider Listing 8-2's ID class whose getNextID() class method returns unique long integer identifiers.

Listing 8-2. Returning Unique Identifiers in a Thread-Safe Manner via `synchronized`

```
class ID
{
   private static volatile long nextID = 1;

   static synchronized long getNextID()
   {
      return nextID++;
   }
}
```

Although the code is properly synchronized (and visibility is accounted for), the intrinsic lock associated with `synchronized` can hurt performance under heavy thread contention. Furthermore, liveness problems such as deadlock can occur. Listing 8-3 shows you how to avoid these problems by replacing `synchronized` with an atomic variable.

Listing 8-3. Returning Unique IDs in a Thread-Safe Manner via `AtomicLong`

```
import java.util.concurrent.atomic.AtomicLong;

class ID
{
   private static AtomicLong nextID = new AtomicLong(1);

   static long getNextID()
   {
      return nextID.getAndIncrement();
   }
}
```

In Listing 8-3, I've converted nextID from a long to an AtomicLong instance, initializing this object to 1. I've also refactored the getNextID() method to call AtomicLong's getAndIncrement() method, which increments the AtomicLong instance's internal long integer variable by 1 and returns the previous value in one indivisible step. There is no explicit synchronization.

■ **Note** The java.util.concurrent.atomic package includes DoubleAccumulator, DoubleAdder, LongAccumulator, and LongAdder classes that address a scalability problem in the context of maintaining a single count, sum, or some other value with the possibility of updates from many threads. These new classes "internally employ contention-reduction techniques that provide huge throughput improvements as compared to atomic variables. This is made possible by relaxing atomicity guarantees in a way that is acceptable in most applications."

Understanding the Atomic Magic

Java's low-level synchronization mechanism, which enforces *mutual exclusion* (the thread holding the lock that guards a set of variables has exclusive access to them) and *visibility* (changes to the guarded variables become visible to other threads that subsequently acquire the lock), impacts hardware utilization and scalability in the following ways:

- *Contended synchronization* (multiple threads constantly competing for a lock) is expensive and throughput suffers as a result. This expense is caused mainly by the frequent *context switching* (switching the central processing unit from one thread to another) that occurs. Each context switch operation can take many processor cycles to complete. In contrast, modern Java virtual machines (JVMs) make *uncontended synchronization* inexpensive.

- When a thread holding a lock is delayed (because of a scheduling delay, for example), no thread that requires that lock makes any progress; the hardware isn't utilized as well as it might be.

Although you might believe that you can use volatile as a synchronization alternative, this won't work. Volatile variables only solve the visibility problem. They cannot be used to safely implement the atomic read-modify-write sequences that are necessary for implementing thread-safe counters and other entities that require mutual exclusion. However, there is an alternative that's responsible for the performance gains offered by the concurrency utilities (such as the java.util.concurrent.Semaphore class). This alternative is known as compare-and-swap.

Compare-and-swap (CAS) is the generic term for an uninterruptible microprocessor-specific instruction that reads a memory location, compares the read value with an expected value, and stores a new value in the memory location when the read value matches the expected value. Otherwise, nothing is done. Modern microprocessors offer variations of CAS. For example, Intel microprocessors provide the cmpxchg family of instructions, whereas the older PowerPC microprocessors provide equivalent load-link (such as lwarx) and store-conditional (such as stwcx) instructions.

CAS supports atomic read-modify-write sequences. You typically use CAS as follows:

1. Read value *x* from address *A*.

2. Perform a multistep computation on *x* to derive a new value called *y*.

3. Use CAS to change the value of *A* from *x* to *y*. CAS succeeds when *A*'s value hasn't changed while performing these steps.

To understand CAS's benefit, consider Listing 8-2's ID class, which returns a unique identifier. Because this class declares its getNextID() method synchronized, high contention for the monitor lock results in excessive context switching that can delay all of the threads and result in an application that doesn't scale well.

Assume the existence of a CAS class that stores an int-based value in value. Furthermore, it offers atomic methods int getValue() for returning value and int compareAndSwap(int expectedValue, int newValue) for implementing CAS. (Behind the scenes, CAS relies on the Java Native Interface [JNI] to access the microprocessor-specific CAS instruction.)

The compareAndSwap() method executes the following instruction sequence atomically:

```
int readValue = value;              // Obtain the stored value.
if (readValue == expectedValue)     // If stored value not modified ...
   value = newValue;                // ... change to new value.
return readValue;                   // Return value before a potential change.
```

Listing 8-4 presents a new version of ID that uses the CAS class to obtain a unique identifier in a highly performant manner. (Forget about the performance ramifications of using the JNI and assume that we had direct access to the microprocessor-specific CAS instruction.)

Listing 8-4. Returning Unique IDs in a Thread-Safe Manner via CAS

```
class ID
{
   private static CAS value = new CAS(1);

   static long getNextID()
   {
      int curValue = value.getValue();
      while (value.compareAndSwap(curValue, curValue + 1) != curValue)
         curValue = value.getValue();
      return curValue - 1;
   }
}
```

ID encapsulates a CAS instance initialized to int-value 1 and declares a getNextID() method for retrieving the current identifier value and then incrementing this value with help from this instance. After retrieving the instance's current value, getNextID() repeatedly invokes compareAndSwap() until curValue's value hasn't changed (by another thread). This method is then free to change this value, after which it returns the previous value. When no lock is involved, contention is avoided along with excessive context switching. Performance improves and the code is more scalable.

As an example of how CAS improves the concurrency utilities, consider java.util.concurrent.locks.ReentrantLock. This class offers better performance than synchronized under high thread contention. To boost performance, ReentrantLock's synchronization is managed by a subclass of the abstract java.util.concurrent.locks. AbstractQueuedSynchronizer class. In turn, this class leverages the undocumented sun.misc.Unsafe class and its compareAndSwapInt() CAS method.

The atomic variable classes also leverage CAS. Furthermore, they provide a method that has the following form:

```
boolean compareAndSet(expectedValue, updateValue)
```

This method (which varies in argument types across different classes) atomically sets a variable to the updateValue when it currently holds the expectedValue, reporting true on success.

Fork/Join Framework

There is always a need for code to execute faster. Historically, this need was met by increasing microprocessor speeds and/or by supporting multiple processors. However, somewhere around 2003, microprocessor speeds stopped increasing because of natural limits. To compensate, processor manufacturers started to add multiple processing cores to their processors, to increase speed through massive parallelism.

■ **Note**   *Parallelism* refers to running threads simultaneously through some combination of multiple processors and cores. In contrast, *concurrency* is a more generalized form of parallelism in which threads run simultaneously or appear to run simultaneously through context switching, also known as *virtual parallelism*. Some people further characterize concurrency as a property of a program or operating system and parallelism as the runtime behavior of executing multiple threads simultaneously.

Java supports concurrency via its low-level threading features and higher-level concurrency utilities such as thread pools. The problem with concurrency is that it doesn't maximize the use of available processor/core resources. For example, suppose you've created a sorting algorithm that divides an array into two halves, assigns two threads to sort each half, and merges the results after both threads finish.

Let's assume that each thread runs on a different processor. Because different amounts of element reordering may occur in each half of the array, it's possible that one thread will finish before the other thread and must wait before the merge can happen. In this case, a processor resource is wasted.

This problem (and the related problems of the code being verbose and harder to read) can be solved by recursively breaking a task into subtasks and combining results. These subtasks run in parallel and complete approximately at the same time (if not at the same moment), where their results are merged and passed up the stack to the previous layer of subtasks. Hardly any processor time is wasted through waiting, and the recursive code is less verbose and (usually) easier to understand. Java provides the Fork/Join Framework to implement this scenario.

Fork/Join consists of a special executor service and thread pool. The executor service makes a task available to the framework, and this task is broken into smaller tasks that are *forked* (executed by different threads) from the pool. A task waits until *joined* (its subtasks finish).

Fork/Join uses *work stealing* to minimize thread contention and overhead. Each worker thread from a pool of worker threads has its own double-ended work queue and pushes new tasks to this queue. It reads the task from the head of the queue. If the queue is empty, the worker thread tries to get a task from the tail of another queue. Stealing is infrequent because worker threads put tasks into their queues in a last-in, first-out (LIFO) order, and the size of work items gets smaller as a problem is divided into subproblems. You start by giving the tasks to a central worker and it keeps dividing them into smaller tasks. Eventually all of the workers have something to do with minimal synchronization.

Fork/Join largely consists of the java.util.concurrent package's ForkJoinPool, ForkJoinTask, ForkJoinWorkerThread, RecursiveAction, RecursiveTask, and CountedCompleter classes:

- ForkJoinPool is a java.util.concurrent.ExecutorService implementation for running ForkJoinTasks. A ForkJoinPool instance provides the entry point for submissions from non-ForkJoinTask clients, as well as providing management and monitoring operations.

- ForkJoinTask is the abstract base class for tasks that run in a ForkJoinPool context. A ForkJoinTask instance is a thread-like entity that is much lighter weight than a normal thread. Huge numbers of tasks and subtasks may be hosted by a small number of actual threads in a ForkJoinPool, at the price of some usage limitations.

- ForkJoinWorkerThread describes a thread managed by a ForkJoinPool instance, which executes ForkJoinTasks.

- RecursiveAction describes a recursive result-less ForkJoinTask.

- RecursiveTask describes a recursive result-bearing ForkJoinTask.

- CountedCompleter describes a ForkJoinTask with a *completion action* (code that completes a fork/join task) performed when triggered and there are no remaining pending actions.

The Java documentation provides examples of RecursiveAction-based tasks (such as sorting) and RecursiveTask-based tasks (such as computing Fibonacci numbers). You can also use RecursiveAction to accomplish matrix multiplication (see http://en.wikipedia.org/wiki/Matrix_multiplication). For example, suppose that you've created Listing 8-5's Matrix class to represent a matrix consisting of a specific number of rows and columns.

Listing 8-5. A Class for Representing a Two-Dimensional Table

```java
public class Matrix
{
   private final int[][] matrix;

   public Matrix(int nrows, int ncols)
   {
      matrix = new int[nrows][ncols];
   }

   public int getCols()
   {
      return matrix[0].length;
   }
```

```
   public int getRows()
   {
      return matrix.length;
   }

   public int getValue(int row, int col)
   {
      return matrix[row][col];
   }

   public void setValue(int row, int col, int value)
   {
      matrix[row][col] = value;
   }
}
```

Listing 8-6 demonstrates the single-threaded approach to multiplying two Matrix instances.

Listing 8-6. Multiplying Two Matrix Instances via the Standard Matrix-Multiplication Algorithm

```
public class MatMult
{
   public static void main(String[] args)
   {
      Matrix a = new Matrix(1, 3);
      a.setValue(0, 0, 1); // | 1 2 3 |
      a.setValue(0, 1, 2);
      a.setValue(0, 2, 3);
      dump(a);
      Matrix b = new Matrix(3, 2);
      b.setValue(0, 0, 4); // | 4 7 |
      b.setValue(1, 0, 5); // | 5 8 |
      b.setValue(2, 0, 6); // | 6 9 |
      b.setValue(0, 1, 7);
      b.setValue(1, 1, 8);
      b.setValue(2, 1, 9);
      dump(b);
      dump(multiply(a, b));
   }
```

```java
    public static void dump(Matrix m)
    {
        for (int i = 0; i < m.getRows(); i++)
        {
            for (int j = 0; j < m.getCols(); j++)
                System.out.printf("%d ", m.getValue(i, j));
            System.out.println();
        }
        System.out.println();
    }

    public static Matrix multiply(Matrix a, Matrix b)
    {
        if (a.getCols() != b.getRows())
            throw new IllegalArgumentException("rows/columns mismatch");
        Matrix result = new Matrix(a.getRows(), b.getCols());
        for (int i = 0; i < a.getRows(); i++)
            for (int j = 0; j < b.getCols(); j++)
                for (int k = 0; k < a.getCols(); k++)
                    result.setValue(i, j, result.getValue(i, j) +
                                    a.getValue(i, k) * b.getValue(k, j));
        return result;
    }
}
```

Listing 8-6's MatMult class declares a multiply() method that demonstrates matrix multiplication. After verifying that the number of columns in the first Matrix (a) equals the number of rows in the second Matrix (b), which is essential to the algorithm, multiply() creates a result Matrix and enters a sequence of nested loops to perform the multiplication.

The essence of these loops is as follows: For each row in a, multiply each of that row's column values by the corresponding column's row values in b. Add the results of the multiplications and store the overall total in result at the location specified via the row index (i) in a and the column index (j) in b.

Compile Listing 8-6 and Listing 8-5, which must be in the same directory, as follows:

```
javac MultMat.java
```

Run the resulting application as follows:

```
java MatMult
```

You should observe the following output, which indicates that a 1-row-by-3-column matrix multiplied by a 3-row-by-2 column matrix results in a 1-row-by-2-column matrix:

```
1 2 3

4 7
5 8
6 9

32 50
```

Computer scientists classify this algorithm as O(n*n*n), which is read "big-oh of n-cubed" or "approximately n-cubed." This notation is an abstract way of classifying the algorithm's performance (without being bogged down in specific details such as microprocessor speed). A O(n*n*n) classification indicates very poor performance, and this performance worsens as the sizes of the matrixes being multiplied increase.

The performance can be improved (on multiprocessor and/or multicore platforms) by assigning each row-by-column multiplication task to a separate thread-like entity. Listing 8-7 shows you how to accomplish this scenario in the context of the Fork/Join Framework.

Listing 8-7. Multiplying Two Matrix Instances with Help from the Fork/Join Framework

```java
import java.util.ArrayList;
import java.util.List;

import java.util.concurrent.ForkJoinPool;
import java.util.concurrent.RecursiveAction;

public class MatMult extends RecursiveAction
{
   private final Matrix a, b, c;
   private final int row;

   public MatMult(Matrix a, Matrix b, Matrix c)
   {
      this(a, b, c, -1);
   }

   public MatMult(Matrix a, Matrix b, Matrix c, int row)
   {
      if (a.getCols() != b.getRows())
         throw new IllegalArgumentException("rows/columns mismatch");
      this.a = a;
      this.b = b;
      this.c = c;
      this.row = row;
   }
```

```java
@Override
public void compute()
{
    if (row == -1)
    {
        List<MatMult> tasks = new ArrayList<>();
        for (int row = 0; row < a.getRows(); row++)
            tasks.add(new MatMult(a, b, c, row));
        invokeAll(tasks);
    }
    else
        multiplyRowByColumn(a, b, c, row);
}

public static void multiplyRowByColumn(Matrix a, Matrix b, Matrix c,
                                       int row)
{
    for (int j = 0; j < b.getCols(); j++)
        for (int k = 0; k < a.getCols(); k++)
            c.setValue(row, j, c.getValue(row, j) +
                        a.getValue(row, k) * b.getValue(k, j));
}

public static void dump(Matrix m)
{
    for (int i = 0; i < m.getRows(); i++)
    {
        for (int j = 0; j < m.getCols(); j++)
            System.out.print(m.getValue(i, j) + " ");
        System.out.println();
    }
    System.out.println();
}

public static void main(String[] args)
{
    Matrix a = new Matrix(2, 3);
    a.setValue(0, 0, 1); // | 1 2 3 |
    a.setValue(0, 1, 2); // | 4 5 6 |
    a.setValue(0, 2, 3);
    a.setValue(1, 0, 4);
    a.setValue(1, 1, 5);
    a.setValue(1, 2, 6);
    dump(a);
    Matrix b = new Matrix(3, 2);
    b.setValue(0, 0, 7); // | 7 1 |
    b.setValue(1, 0, 8); // | 8 2 |
```

```
        b.setValue(2, 0, 9); // | 9 3 |
        b.setValue(0, 1, 1);
        b.setValue(1, 1, 2);
        b.setValue(2, 1, 3);
        dump(b);
        Matrix c = new Matrix(2, 2);
        ForkJoinPool pool = new ForkJoinPool();
        pool.invoke(new MatMult(a, b, c));
        dump(c);
    }
}
```

Listing 8-7 presents a MatMult class that extends RecursiveAction. To accomplish meaningful work, RecursiveAction's void compute() method is overridden.

■ **Note** Although compute() is normally used to subdivide a task into subtasks recursively, I've chosen to handle the multiplication task somewhat differently (for brevity and simplicity).

After creating Matrixes a and b, Listing 8-7's main() method creates Matrix c and instantiates ForkJoinPool. It then instantiates MatMult, passing these three Matrix instances as arguments to the MatMult(Matrix a, Matrix b, Matrix c) constructor, and calls ForkJoinPool's T invoke(ForkJoinTask<T> task) method to start running this initial task. This method doesn't return until the initial task and all of its subtasks complete.

The MatMult(Matrix a, Matrix b, Matrix c) constructor invokes the MatMult(Matrix a, Matrix b, Matrix c, int row) constructor, specifying -1 as row's value. This value is used by compute(), which is invoked as a result of the aforementioned invoke() method call, to distinguish between the initial task and subtasks.

When compute() is initially called (row equals -1), it creates a List of MatMult tasks and passes this List to RecursiveAction's Collection<T> invokeAll(Collection<T> tasks) method (inherited from ForkJoinTask). This method forks all of the List collection's tasks, which will start to execute. It then waits until the invokeAll() method returns (which also joins to all of these tasks), which happens when the boolean isDone() method (also inherited from ForkJoinTask) returns true for each task.

Notice the tasks.add(new MatMult(a, b, c, row)); method call. This call assigns a specific row value to a MatMult instance. When invokeAll() is called, each task's compute() method is called and detects a different value (other than -1) assigned to row. It then executes multiplyRowByColumn(a, b, c, row); for its specific row.

Compile Listing 8-7 (javac MatMult.java) and run the resulting application (java MatMult). You should observe the following output:

```
1 2 3
4 5 6

7 1
8 2
9 3

50 14
122 32
```

Completion Services

A *completion service* is an implementation of the java.util.concurrent. CompletionService<V> interface that decouples the production of new asynchronous tasks (a producer) from the consumption of the results of completed tasks (a consumer). V is the type of a task result.

A producer submits a task for execution (via a worker thread) by calling one of the submit() methods: one method accepts a callable argument and the other method accepts a runnable argument along with a result to return upon task completion. Each method returns a Future<V> instance that represents the pending completion of the task. You can then call a poll() method to poll for the task's completion or call the blocking take() method.

A consumer takes a completed task by calling the take() method. This method blocks until a task has completed. It then returns a Future<V> object that represents the completed task. You would call Future<V>'s get() method to obtain this result.

Along with CompletionService<V>, Java 7 introduced the java.util.concurrent. ExecutorCompletionService<V> class to support task execution via a provided executor. This class ensures that, when submitted tasks are complete, they are placed on a queue that's accessible to take().

To demonstrate CompletionService and ExecutorCompletionService, I'm revisiting the application for calculating Euler's number that I first presented in Chapter 5. Listing 8-8 presents the source code to a new application that submits two callable tasks to calculate this number to different accuracies.

Listing 8-8. Calculating Euler's Number via a Completion Service

```java
import java.math.BigDecimal;
import java.math.MathContext;
import java.math.RoundingMode;

import java.util.concurrent.Callable;
import java.util.concurrent.CompletionService;
import java.util.concurrent.ExecutorCompletionService;
import java.util.concurrent.Executors;
import java.util.concurrent.ExecutorService;
import java.util.concurrent.Future;
```

```java
public class CSDemo
{
   public static void main(String[] args) throws Exception
   {
      ExecutorService es = Executors.newFixedThreadPool(10);
      CompletionService<BigDecimal> cs =
         new ExecutorCompletionService<BigDecimal>(es);
      cs.submit(new CalculateE(17));
      cs.submit(new CalculateE(170));
      Future<BigDecimal> result = cs.take();
      System.out.println(result.get());
      System.out.println();
      result = cs.take();
      System.out.println(result.get());
      es.shutdown();
   }
}

class CalculateE implements Callable<BigDecimal>
{
   final int lastIter;

   public CalculateE(int lastIter)
   {
      this.lastIter = lastIter;
   }

   @Override
   public BigDecimal call()
   {
      MathContext mc = new MathContext(100, RoundingMode.HALF_UP);
      BigDecimal result = BigDecimal.ZERO;
      for (int i = 0; i <= lastIter; i++)
      {
         BigDecimal factorial = factorial(new BigDecimal(i));
         BigDecimal res = BigDecimal.ONE.divide(factorial, mc);
         result = result.add(res);
      }
      return result;
   }

   private BigDecimal factorial(BigDecimal n)
   {
      if (n.equals(BigDecimal.ZERO))
         return BigDecimal.ONE;
      else
         return n.multiply(factorial(n.subtract(BigDecimal.ONE)));
   }
}
```

Listing 8-8 presents two classes: CSDemo and CalculateE. CSDemo drives the application and CalculateE describes the Euler's number calculation task.

CSDemo's main() method first creates an executor service that will execute a task. It then creates a completion service for completing the task. Two calculation tasks are subsequently submitted to the completion service, which runs each task asynchronously. For each task, the completion service's take() method is called to return the task's future, whose get() method is called to obtain the task result, which is then output.

CalculateE contains code that's nearly identical to what was presented in Chapter 5 (see Listing 5-1). The only difference is the change from a LASTITER constant to a lastIter variable that records the last iteration to execute (and determines the number of digits of precision).

Compile Listing 8-8 as follows:

```
javac CSDemo.java
```

Run the resulting application as follows:

```
java CSDemo
```

You should observe the following output:

```
2.71828182845904507051604779584860506117897963525103269890073500406522504250
48433140558879743442457417300039454062711
```

```
2.71828182845904523536028747135266249775724709369995957496696762772407663035
35475945713821785251664274638961162816541248130487298653803083054255562838245
91346003267514458191156049421052628685648847691963042847034916777068481221266
64838550045128841929851772268853216753574895628940347880297133296754744949375
83500554228384631452841986384050112497204406928225548432766806207414980593297
8161481951711991448146506
```

■ **Note** If you're wondering about the difference between an executor service and a completion service, consider that, with an executor service, after writing the code to submit the tasks, you need to write code to efficiently retrieve task results. With a completion service, this job is pretty much automated. Another way to look at these constructs is that an executor service provides an incoming queue for tasks and provides workers threads, whereas a completion service provides an incoming queue for tasks, worker threads, and an output queue for storing task results.

EXERCISES

The following exercises are designed to test your understanding of Chapter 8's content:

1. Identify the two problems with thread-safe collections.

2. Define concurrent collection.

3. What is a weakly-consistent iterator?

4. Describe the `BlockingQueue` interface.

5. Describe the `ConcurrentMap` interface.

6. Describe the `ArrayBlockingQueue` and `LinkedBlockingQueue` `BlockingQueue`-implementation classes.

7. True or false: The concurrency-oriented collection types are part of the Collections Framework.

8. Describe the `ConcurrentHashMap` class.

9. Using `ConcurrentHashMap`, how would you check if a map contains a specific value and, when this value is absent, put this value into the map without relying on external synchronization?

10. Define atomic variable.

11. What does the `AtomicIntegerArray` class describe?

12. True or false: `volatile` supports atomic read-modify-write sequences.

13. What's responsible for the performance gains offered by the concurrency utilities?

14. Describe the Fork/Join Framework.

15. Identify the main types that comprise the Fork/Join Framework.

16. To accomplish meaningful work via `RecursiveAction`, which one of its methods would you override?

17. Define completion service.

18. How do you use a completion service?

19. How do you execute tasks via a completion service?

20. Convert the following expressions to their atomic variable equivalents:

```
int total = ++counter;
int total = counter--;
```

Summary

This chapter completed my tour of the concurrency utilities by introducing concurrent collections, atomic variables, the Fork/Join Framework, and completion services.

A concurrent collection is a concurrency performant and highly-scalable collections-oriented type that is stored in the java.util.concurrent package. It overcomes the ConcurrentModificationException and performance problems of thread-safe collections.

An atomic variable is an instance of a class that encapsulates a single variable and supports lock-free, thread-safe operations on that variable, for example, AtomicInteger.

The Fork/Join Framework consists of a special executor service and thread pool. The executor service makes a task available to the framework, and this task is broken down into smaller tasks that are forked (executed by different threads) from the pool. A task waits until it's joined (its subtasks finish).

A completion service is an implementation of the CompletionService<V> interface that decouples the production of new asynchronous tasks (a producer) from the consumption of the results of completed tasks (a consumer). V is the type of a task result.

Appendix A presents the answers to each chapter's exercises.

PART III

Appendices

■ ■ ■

Answers to Exercises

Each of Chapters 1 through 8 closes with an "Exercises" section that tests your understanding of the chapter's material. The answers to those exercises are presented in this appendix.

Chapter 1: Threads and Runnables

1. A thread is an independent path of execution through an application's code.

2. A runnable is a code sequence encapsulated into an object whose class implements the Runnable interface.

3. The Thread class provides a consistent interface to the underlying operating system's threading architecture. The Runnable interface supplies the code to be executed by the thread that's associated with a Thread object.

4. The two ways to create a Runnable object are to instantiate an anonymous class that implements the Runnable interface and to use a lambda expression.

5. The two ways to connect a runnable to a Thread object are to pass the runnable to a Thread constructor that accepts a runnable argument and to subclass Thread and override its void run() method when the constructor doesn't accept a runnable argument. Thread implements the Runnable interface, which makes Thread objects runnables as well.

6. The five kinds of Thread state are a name, an indication of whether the thread is alive or dead, the execution state of the thread (is it runnable?), the thread's priority, and an indication of whether the thread is daemon or nondaemon.

7. The answer is false: a default thread name starts with the Thread- prefix.

8. You give a thread a nondefault name by calling a `Thread` constructor that accepts a thread name or by calling `Thread`'s `void setName(String name)` method.

9. You determine if a thread is alive or dead by calling `Thread`'s `boolean isAlive()` method.

10. The `Thread.State` enum's constants are `NEW` (a thread that has not yet started is in this state), `RUNNABLE` (a thread executing in the Java virtual machine [JVM] is in this state), `BLOCKED` (a thread that is blocked waiting for a monitor lock is in this state), `WAITING` (a thread that is waiting indefinitely for another thread to perform a particular action is in this state), `TIMED_WAITING` (a thread that is waiting for another thread to perform an action for up to a specified waiting time is in this state), and `TERMINATED` (a thread that has exited is in this state).

11. You obtain the current thread execution state by calling `Thread`'s `Thread.State getState()` method.

12. Priority is thread-relative importance.

13. Using `setPriority()` can impact an application's portability across operating systems because different schedulers can handle a priority change in different ways.

14. The range of values that you can pass to `Thread`'s `void setPriority(int priority)` method are `Thread.MIN_PRIORITY` to `Thread.MAX_PRIORITY`.

15. The answer is true: a daemon thread dies automatically when the application's last nondaemon thread dies so that the application can terminate.

16. `Thread`'s `void start()` method throws `IllegalThreadStateException` when called on a `Thread` object whose thread is running or has died.

17. You would stop an unending application on Windows by pressing the Ctrl and C keys simultaneously.

18. The methods that form `Thread`'s interruption mechanism are `void interrupt()`, `static boolean interrupted()`, and `boolean isInterrupted()`.

19. The answer is false: the `boolean isInterrupted()` method doesn't clear the interrupted status of this thread. The interrupted status is unaffected.

20. A thread throws `InterruptedException` when it's interrupted.

21. A busy loop is a loop of statements designed to waste some time.

22. Thread's methods that let a thread wait for another thread to die are void join(), void join(long millis), and void join(long millis, int nanos).

23. Thread's methods that let a thread sleep are void sleep(long millis) and void sleep(long millis, int nanos).

24. Listing A-1 presents the IntSleep application that was called for in Chapter 1.

Listing A-1. Interrupting a Sleeping Background Thread

```java
public class IntSleep
{
    public static void main(String[] args)
    {
        Runnable r = new Runnable()
                     {
                         @Override
                         public void run()
                         {
                             while (true)
                             {
                                 System.out.println("hello");
                                 try
                                 {
                                     Thread.sleep(100);
                                 }
                                 catch (InterruptedException ie)
                                 {
                                     System.out.println("interrupted");
                                     break;
                                 }
                             }
                         }
                     };
        Thread t = new Thread(r);
        t.start();
        try
        {
            Thread.sleep(2000);
        }
        catch (InterruptedException ie)
        {
        }
        t.interrupt();
    }
}
```

Chapter 2: Synchronization

1. The three problems with threads are race conditions, data races, and cached variables.

2. The answer is false: when the correctness of a computation depends on the relative timing or interleaving of multiple threads by the scheduler, you have a race condition.

3. Synchronization is a JVM feature that ensures that two or more concurrent threads don't simultaneously execute a critical section.

4. The two properties of synchronization are mutual exclusion and visibility.

5. Synchronization is implemented in terms of monitors, which are concurrency constructs for controlling access to critical sections, which must execute indivisibly. Each Java object is associated with a monitor, which a thread can lock or unlock acquiring and releasing the monitor's lock token.

6. The answer is true: a thread that has acquired a lock doesn't release this lock when it calls one of Thread's sleep() methods.

7. You specify a synchronized method by including the keyword synchronized in the method header.

8. You specify a synchronized block by specifying the syntax synchronized(*object*) {}.

9. Liveness refers to something beneficial happening eventually.

10. The three liveness challenges are deadlock, livelock, and starvation (also known as indefinite postponement).

11. The volatile keyword differs from synchronized in that volatile deals with visibility only, whereas synchronized deals with mutual exclusion and visibility.

12. The answer is true: Java also lets you safely access a final field without the need for synchronization.

13. The thread problems with the CheckingAccount class are the check-then-act race condition in the withdraw() method between if (amount <= balance) and balance -= amount; (which results in more money being withdrawn than is available for withdrawal) and the potentially cached balance field. The balance field can be cached on multiprocessor/ multicore systems and the cached copy used by the withdrawal thread might not contain the initial balance set in the constructor by the default main thread.

14. Listing A-2 presents the CheckingAccount application that was called for in Chapter 2.

Listing A-2. Fixing a Problematic Checking Account

```java
public class CheckingAccount
{
   private volatile int balance;

   public CheckingAccount(int initialBalance)
   {
      balance = initialBalance;
   }

   public synchronized boolean withdraw(int amount)
   {
      if (amount <= balance)
      {
         try
         {
            Thread.sleep((int) (Math.random() * 200));
         }
         catch (InterruptedException ie)
         {
         }
         balance -= amount;
         return true;
      }
      return false;
   }

   public static void main(String[] args)
   {
      final CheckingAccount ca = new CheckingAccount(100);
      Runnable r = new Runnable()
                  {
                     @Override
                     public void run()
                     {
                        String name = Thread.currentThread().getName();
                        for (int i = 0; i < 10; i++)
                           System.out.println (name + " withdraws $10: " +
                                               ca.withdraw(10));
                     }
                  };
      Thread thdHusband = new Thread(r);
      thdHusband.setName("Husband");
      Thread thdWife = new Thread(r);
      thdWife.setName("Wife");
      thdHusband.start();
      thdWife.start();
   }
}
```

This application uses `volatile` to deal with potential cache problems and synchronized to deal with the need for mutual exclusion.

Chapter 3: Waiting and Notification

1. A condition is a prerequisite for continued execution.

2. The API that supports conditions consists of Object's three `wait()` methods, one `notify()` method, and one `notifyAll()` method. The `wait()` methods wait for a condition to exist; the `notify()` and `notifyAll()` methods notify the waiting thread when the condition exists.

3. The answer is true: the `wait()` methods are interruptible.

4. You would call the `notifyAll()` method to wake up all threads that are waiting on an object's monitor.

5. The answer is false: a thread that has acquired a lock releases this lock when it calls one of Object's `wait()` methods.

6. A condition queue is a data structure that stores threads waiting for a condition to exist. The waiting threads are known as the wait set.

7. When you call any of the API's methods outside of a synchronized context, `IllegalMonitorStateException` is thrown.

8. A spurious wakeup is a thread waking up without being notified, interrupted, or timing out.

9. You should call a `wait()` method in a loop context to ensure liveness and safety.

10. Listing A-3 presents the `Await` application that was called for in Chapter 3.

Listing A-3. Using `wait()` and `notifyAll()` to Create a Higher-Level Concurrency Construct

```
public class Await
{
    static volatile int count;

    public static void main(String[] args)
    {
        Runnable r = () ->
                     {
                         Thread curThread = Thread.currentThread();
                         System.out.printf("%s has entered runnable and is " +
```

```
                                        "waiting%n", curThread.getName());
                    synchronized(Await.class)
                    {
                        count++;
                        try
                        {
                            Thread.sleep(2000);
                            while (count < 3)
                                Await.class.wait();
                        }
                        catch (InterruptedException ie)
                        {
                        }
                    }
                    System.out.printf("%s has woken up and is " +
                                      "terminating%n",
                                      curThread.getName());
                };
        Thread thdA = new Thread(r, "thdA");
        Thread thdB = new Thread(r, "thdB");
        Thread thdC = new Thread(r, "thdC");
        thdA.start();
        thdB.start();
        thdC.start();
        r = new Runnable()
                {
                    @Override
                    public void run()
                    {
                        try
                        {
                            while (count < 3)
                                Thread.sleep(100);
                            synchronized(Await.class)
                            {
                                Await.class.notifyAll();
                            }
                        }
                        catch (InterruptedException ie)
                        {
                        }
                    }
                };
        Thread thd = new Thread(r);
        thd.start();
    }
}
```

Chapter 4: Additional Thread Capabilities

1. A thread group is a set of threads. It's represented by the ThreadGroup class.

2. You might use a thread group to perform a common operation on its threads, to simplify thread management.

3. You should avoid using thread groups because the most useful ThreadGroup methods have been deprecated and because of the "time of check to time of use" race condition between obtaining a count of active threads and enumerating those threads.

4. You should be aware of thread groups because of ThreadGroup's contribution in handling exceptions that are thrown while a thread is executing.

5. A thread-local variable is a variable that provides a separate storage slot to each thread that accesses the variable. It's represented by the ThreadLocal class.

6. The answer is true: if an entry doesn't exist in the calling thread's storage slot when the thread calls get(), this method calls initialValue().

7. You would pass a value from a parent thread to a child thread by working with the InheritableThreadLocal class.

8. The classes that form the Timer Framework are Timer and TimerTask.

9. The answer is false: Timer() creates a new timer whose task-execution thread runs as a nondaemon thread.

10. In fixed-delay execution, each execution is scheduled relative to the actual execution time of the previous execution. When an execution is delayed for any reason (such as garbage collection), subsequent executions are also delayed.

11. You call the schedule() methods to schedule a task for fixed-delay execution.

12. In fixed-rate execution, each execution is scheduled relative to the scheduled execution time of the initial execution. When an execution is delayed for any reason (such as garbage collection), two or more executions will occur in rapid succession to "catch up."

13. The difference between Timer's cancel() method and TimerTask's cancel() method is as follows: Timer's cancel() method terminates the timer, discarding any currently scheduled timer tasks. In contrast, TimerTask's cancel() method cancels the invoking timer task only.

14. Listing A-4 presents the BackAndForth application that was called for in Chapter 4.

Listing A-4. Repeatedly Moving an Asterisk Back and Forth via a Timer

```java
import java.util.Timer;
import java.util.TimerTask;

public class BackAndForth
{
   static enum Direction { FORWARDS, BACKWARDS }

   public static void main(String[] args)
   {
      TimerTask task = new TimerTask()
                       {
                          final static int MAXSTEPS = 20;

                          volatile Direction direction = Direction.FORWARDS;

                          volatile int steps = 0;

                          @Override
                          public void run()
                          {
                             switch (direction)
                             {
                                case FORWARDS : System.out.print("\b ");
                                                System.out.print("*");
                                                break;

                                case BACKWARDS: System.out.print("\b ");
                                                System.out.print("\b\b*");
                             }
```

```
                    if (++steps == MAXSTEPS)
                    {
                        direction =
                            (direction == Direction.FORWARDS)
                            ? Direction.BACKWARDS
                            : Direction.FORWARDS;
                        steps = 0;
                    }
                }
            };
    Timer timer = new Timer();
    timer.schedule(task, 0, 100);
    }
}
```

Chapter 5: Concurrency Utilities and Executors

1. The concurrency utilities are a framework of classes and interfaces that overcome problems with Java's low-level thread capabilities. Specifically, low-level concurrency primitives such as synchronized and wait()/notify() are often hard to use correctly, too much reliance on the synchronized primitive can lead to performance issues, which affect an application's scalability, and higher-level constructs such as thread pools and semaphores aren't included with Java's low-level thread capabilities.

2. The packages in which the concurrency utilities types are stored are java.util.concurrent, java.util.concurrent.atomic, and java.util.concurrent.locks.

3. A task is an object whose class implements the Runnable interface (a runnable task) or the Callable interface (a callable task).

4. An executor is an object whose class directly or indirectly implements the Executor interface, which decouples task submission from task-execution mechanics.

5. The Executor interface focuses exclusively on Runnable, which means that there's no convenient way for a runnable task to return a value to its caller (because Runnable's run() method doesn't return a value); Executor doesn't provide a way to track the progress of executing runnable tasks, cancel an executing runnable task, or determine when the runnable task finishes execution; Executor cannot execute a collection of runnable tasks; and Executor doesn't provide a way for an application to shut down an executor (much less to properly shut down an executor).

6. Executor's limitations are overcome by providing the ExecutorService interface.

7. The differences existing between Runnable's run() method and Callable's call() method are as follows: run() cannot return a value, whereas call() can return a value; and run() cannot throw checked exceptions, whereas call() can throw checked exceptions.

8. The answer is false: you can throw checked and unchecked exceptions from Callable's call() method but can only throw unchecked exceptions from Runnable's run() method.

9. A future is an object whose class implements the Future interface. It represents an asynchronous computation and provides methods for canceling a task, for returning a task's value, and for determining whether or not the task has finished.

10. The Executors class's newFixedThreadPool() method creates a thread pool that reuses a fixed number of threads operating off of a shared unbounded queue. At most, nThreads threads are actively processing tasks. If additional tasks are submitted when all threads are active, they wait in the queue for an available thread. If any thread terminates because of a failure during execution before the executor shuts down, a new thread will take its place when needed to execute subsequent tasks. The threads in the pool will exist until the executor is explicitly shut down.

11. Listing A-5 presents the CountingThreads application that was called for in Chapter 5.

Listing A-5. Executor-Based Counting Threads

```java
import java.util.concurrent.Executors;
import java.util.concurrent.ExecutorService;

public class CountingThreads
{
   public static void main(String[] args)
   {
      Runnable r = new Runnable()
                   {
                      @Override
                      public void run()
                      {
                         String name = Thread.currentThread().getName();
                         int count = 0;
                         while (true)
```

```
                                System.out.println(name + ": " + count++);
                        }
                };
        ExecutorService es = Executors.newFixedThreadPool(2);
        es.submit(r);
        es.submit(r);
    }
}
```

12. Listing A-6 presents the CountingThreads application with custom-named threads that was called for in Chapter 5.

Listing A-6. Executor-Based Counting Threads A and B

```java
import java.util.concurrent.Executors;
import java.util.concurrent.ExecutorService;
import java.util.concurrent.ThreadFactory;

public class CountingThreads
{
    public static void main(String[] args)
    {
        Runnable r = new Runnable()
                    {
                        @Override
                        public void run()
                        {
                            String name = Thread.currentThread().getName();
                            int count = 0;
                            while (true)
                                System.out.println(name + ": " + count++);
                        }
                    };
        ExecutorService es =
            Executors.newSingleThreadExecutor(new NamedThread("A"));
        es.submit(r);
        es = Executors.newSingleThreadExecutor(new NamedThread("B"));
        es.submit(r);
    }
}

class NamedThread implements ThreadFactory
{
    private volatile String name; // newThread() could be called by a
                                  // different thread
```

```
NamedThread(String name)
{
    this.name = name;
}

@Override
public Thread newThread(Runnable r)
{
    return new Thread(r, name);
}
}
```

Chapter 6: Synchronizers

1. A synchronizer is a class that facilitates a common form of synchronization.

2. A countdown latch causes one or more threads to wait at a "gate" until another thread opens this gate, at which point these other threads can continue. It consists of a count and operations for "causing a thread to wait until the count reaches zero" and "decrementing the count".

3. When CountDownLatch's void countDown() method is called and the count reaches zero, all waiting threads are released.

4. A cyclic barrier lets a set of threads wait for each other to reach a common barrier point. The barrier is cyclic because it can be reused after the waiting threads are released. This synchronizer is useful in applications involving a fixed-size party of threads that must occasionally wait for each other.

5. The answer is false: CyclicBarrier's int await() method throws BrokenBarrierException when the barrier is reset while any thread is waiting or when the barrier is broken when await() is invoked.

6. An exchanger provides a synchronization point where threads can swap objects. Each thread presents some object on entry to the exchanger's exchange() method, matches with a partner thread, and receives its partner's object on return.

7. Exchanger's V exchange(V x) method waits for another thread to arrive at this exchange point (unless the calling thread is interrupted), and then transfers the given object to it, receiving the other thread's object in return.

8. A semaphore maintains a set of permits for restricting the number of threads that can access a limited resource. A thread attempting to acquire a permit when no permits are available blocks until some other thread releases a permit.

9. The two kinds of semaphores are counting semaphores (the current values can be incremented past 1) and binary semaphores or mutexs (the current values can be only 0 or 1).

10. A phaser is a more flexible cyclic barrier. Like a cyclic barrier, a phaser lets a group of threads wait on a barrier; these threads continue after the last thread arrives. A phaser also offers the equivalent of a barrier action. Unlike a cyclic barrier, which coordinates a fixed number of threads, a phaser can coordinate a variable number of threads, which can register at any time. To implement this capability, a phaser uses phases (current states) and phase numbers (current state identifiers).

11. Phaser's int register() method returns the phase number to classify the arrival. If this value is negative, this phaser has terminated, in which case registration has no effect. This number is known as the arrival phase number.

12. Listing A-7 presents the PC application that was called for in Chapter 6.

Listing A-7. Semaphore-Based Producer and Consumer

```java
import java.util.concurrent.Semaphore;

public class PC
{
   public static void main(String[] args)
   {
      Shared s = new Shared();
      Semaphore semCon = new Semaphore(0);
      Semaphore semPro = new Semaphore(1);
      new Producer(s, semPro, semCon).start();
      new Consumer(s, semPro, semCon).start();
   }
}

class Shared
{
   private char c;

   void setSharedChar(char c)
   {
      this.c = c;
   }
```

```
   char getSharedChar()
   {
      return c;
   }
}


class Producer extends Thread
{
   private final Shared s;
   private final Semaphore semPro, semCon;

   Producer(Shared s, Semaphore semPro, Semaphore semCon)
   {
      this.s = s;
      this.semPro = semPro;
      this.semCon = semCon;
   }

   @Override
   public void run()
   {
      for (char ch = 'A'; ch <= 'Z'; ch++)
      {
         try
         {
            semPro.acquire();
         }
         catch (InterruptedException ie)
         {
         }
         s.setSharedChar(ch);
         System.out.println(ch + " produced by producer.");
         semCon.release();
      }
   }
}
class Consumer extends Thread
{
   private final Shared s;
   private final Semaphore semPro, semCon;

   Consumer(Shared s, Semaphore semPro, Semaphore semCon)
   {
      this.s = s;
      this.semPro = semPro;
      this.semCon = semCon;
   }
```

```
@Override
public void run()
{
   char ch;
   do
   {
      try
      {
         semCon.acquire();
      }
      catch (InterruptedException ie)
      {
      }
      ch = s.getSharedChar();
      System.out.println(ch + " consumed by consumer.");
      semPro.release();
   }
   while (ch != 'Z');
}
}
```

Chapter 7: The Locking Framework

1. A lock is an instance of a class that implements the Lock interface, which provides more extensive locking operations than can be achieved via the synchronized reserved word. Lock also supports a wait/notification mechanism through associated Condition objects.

2. The biggest advantage that Lock objects hold over the intrinsic locks that are obtained when threads enter critical sections (controlled via the synchronized reserved word) is their ability to back out of an attempt to acquire a lock.

3. The answer is true: ReentrantLock's unlock() method throws IllegalMonitorStateException when the calling thread doesn't hold the lock.

4. You obtain a Condition instance for use with a particular Lock instance by invoking Lock's Condition newCondition() method.

5. The answer is false: ReentrantReadWriteLock() creates an instance of ReentrantReadWriteLock without a fair ordering policy.

6. Introduced by JDK 8, StampedLock is a capability-based lock with three modes for controlling read/write access. It differentiates between exclusive and nonexclusive locks in a manner that's similar to ReentrantReadWriteLock, but also allows for optimistic reads, which ReentrantReadWriteLock doesn't support.

7. The purpose of LockSupport is to provide basic thread-blocking primitives for creating locks and other synchronization classes.

8. Listing A-8 presents the ID class that was called for in Chapter 7.

Listing A-8. ReentrantLock-Based ID Generator

```java
import java.util.concurrent.locks.ReentrantLock;

public class ID
{
   private static int counter; // initialized to 0 by default

   private final static ReentrantLock lock = new ReentrantLock();

   public static int getID()
   {
      lock.lock();
      try
      {
         int temp = counter + 1;
         try
         {
            Thread.sleep(1);
         }
         catch (InterruptedException ie)
         {
         }
         return counter = temp;
      }
      finally
      {
         lock.unlock();
      }
   }
}
```

Chapter 8: Additional Concurrency Utilities

1.   The two problems with thread-safe collections are the possibility of thrown `ConcurrentModificationException` objects and poor performance. It's necessary to acquire a lock before iterating over a collection that might be modified by another thread during the iteration. If a lock isn't acquired and the collection is modified, it's highly likely that `ConcurrentModificationException` will be thrown. Also, performance suffers when synchronized collections are accessed frequently from multiple threads.

2.   A concurrent collection is a concurrency performant and highly-scalable collection-oriented type that is stored in the `java.util.concurrent` package.

3.   A weakly-consistent iterator is an iterator with the following properties:

   • An element that's removed after iteration starts but hasn't yet been returned via the iterator's `next()` method won't be returned.

   • An element that's added after iteration starts may or may not be returned.

   • No element is returned more than once during the iteration of a collection, regardless of changes made to the collection during iteration.

4.   `BlockingQueue` is a subinterface of `java.util.Queue` that also supports blocking operations that wait for the queue to become nonempty before retrieving an element and wait for space to become available in the queue before storing an element.

5.   `ConcurrentMap` is a subinterface of `java.util.Map` that declares additional indivisible `putIfAbsent()`, `remove()`, and `replace()` methods.

6.   `ArrayBlockingQueue` is a bounded blocking queue backed by an array. `LinkedBlockingQueue` is an optionally-bounded blocking queue based on linked nodes.

7.   The answer is true: the concurrency-oriented collection types are part of the Collections Framework.

8.   `ConcurrentHashMap` behaves like `HashMap` but has been designed to work in multithreaded contexts without the need for explicit synchronization.

9. Using `ConcurrentHashMap`, you would call its `putIfAbsent()` method to check if a map contains a specific value and, when this value is absent, put this value into the map without relying on external synchronization.

10. An atomic variable is an instance of a class that encapsulates a single variable and supports lock-free, thread-safe operations on that variable, for example, `AtomicInteger`.

11. The `AtomicIntegerArray` class describes an `int` array whose elements may be updated atomically.

12. The answer is false: `volatile` doesn't support atomic read-modify-write sequences.

13. The compare-and-swap instruction is responsible for the performance gains offered by the concurrency utilities.

14. The Fork/Join Framework consists of a special executor service and thread pool. The executor service makes a task available to the framework, and this task is broken down into smaller tasks that are forked (executed by different threads) from the pool. A task waits until it's joined (its subtasks finish).

15. The main types that comprise the Fork/Join Framework are the `java.util.concurrent` package's `ForkJoinPool`, `ForkJoinTask`, `ForkJoinWorkerThread`, `RecursiveAction`, `RecursiveTask`, and `CountedCompleter` classes.

16. To accomplish meaningful work via `RecursiveAction`, you would override its `void compute()` method.

17. A completion service is an implementation of the `CompletionService<V>` interface that decouples the production of new asynchronous tasks (a producer) from the consumption of the results of completed tasks (a consumer). V is the type of a task result.

18. You use a completion service as follows: Submit a task for execution (via a worker thread) by calling one of `CompletionService<V>`'s `submit()` methods. Each method returns a `Future<V>` instance that represents the pending completion of the task. You can then call a `poll()` method to poll for the task's completion or call the blocking `take()` method. A consumer takes a completed task by calling the `take()` method. This method blocks until a task has completed. It then returns a `Future<V>` object that represents the completed task. You would call `Future<V>`'s `get()` method to obtain this result.

19. You execute tasks via a completion service by working with the ExecutorCompletionService<V> class, which implements CompletionService<V>, and which supports task execution via a provided executor.

20. The atomic variable equivalent of int total = ++counter; is as follows:

```
AtomicInteger counter = new AtomicInteger(0);
int total = counter.incrementAndGet();
```

The atomic variable equivalent of int total = counter--; is as follows:

```
AtomicInteger counter = new AtomicInteger(0);
int total = counter.getAndDecrement();
```

APPENDIX B

■ ■ ■

Threading in Swing

Swing is a platform-independent, Model-View-Controller-based GUI toolkit for creating the graphical frontends of Java applications. In this appendix, I first explore Swing's threading architecture and then explore Swing APIs for avoiding problems when additional threads are used in graphical contexts. Finally, I present a Swing-based slide show application as a significant example of this appendix's content and as a fun way to end this book.

■ **Note** I'll assume that you have some experience with Swing APIs along with the architecture of a Swing application.

A Single-Threaded Programming Model

Swing follows a single-threaded programming model. It's designed to be single-threaded instead of multithreaded because experience in the design of multithreaded graphical toolkits has shown that they inevitably lead to deadlock and race conditions. To learn more about these problems, check out the "Why are GUIs Single-threaded?" blog post (http://codeidol.com/java/java-concurrency/GUI-Applications/Why-are-GUIs-Single-threaded/).

The thread that's used to render graphics and handle events is known as the *event-dispatch thread (EDT)*. The EDT processes events that originate from the underlying Abstract Window Toolkit's event queue and invokes GUI component (such as button) event listeners, which handle events on this thread. Components even redraw themselves (in response to paint() method calls that result in paintComponent(), paintBorder(), and paintChildren() method calls) on the EDT.

Be careful about how your code interacts with the EDT to ensure that your Swing applications work correctly. There are two rules to remember:

- Always create Swing GUIs on the EDT.
- Never delay the EDT.

One consequence of Swing being single-threaded is that you must create a Swing application's GUI on the EDT only. It's incorrect to create this GUI on any other thread, including the default main thread that runs a Java application's main() method.

Most Swing objects (such as javax.swing.JFrame objects, which describe GUI top-level "frame" windows with menu bars and borders) are not thread-safe. Accessing these objects from multiple threads risks thread interference and/or memory inconsistency errors:

- *Thread interference*: Two threads are performing two different operations while acting on the same data. For example, one thread reads a long integer counter variable while another thread updates this variable. Because a long integer being read from or written to on a 32-bit machine requires two read/write accesses, it's possible that the reading thread reads part of this variable's current value, then the writing thread updates the variable, and then the reading thread reads the rest of the variable. The result is that the reading thread has an incorrect value.

- *Memory inconsistency errors*: Two or more threads that are running on different processors or processor cores have inconsistent views of the same data. For example, a writing thread on one processor or core updates a counter variable and then a reading thread on another processor or core reads this variable. However, because a caching mechanism is used to boost performance, neither thread accesses a single copy of the variable in main memory. Instead, each thread accesses its own copy of the variable from local memory (a cache).

How might these problems occur when the GUI isn't created on the EDT? John Zukowski demonstrates one scenario in his *JavaWorld* article titled "Swing threading and the event-dispatch thread" (www.javaworld.com/article/2077754/core-java/swing-threading-and-the-event-dispatch-thread.html).

Zukowski presents an example that adds a container listener to a frame window container component. Listener methods are called when a component is added to or removed from the frame. He demonstrates the EDT running code within a listener method before the frame window is realized on the default main thread.

■ **Note** To be *realized* means that a component's paint() method either has been called or might be called. A frame window is realized by having one of setVisible(true), show(), or pack() called on this container component. After a frame window is realized, all of the components that it contains are also realized. Another way to realize a component is to add it to a container that's already realized.

After the EDT starts to run in a listener method, and while the default main thread continues to initialize the GUI, components could be created by the default main thread and accessed by the EDT. The EDT might try to access these components before they exist; doing so could crash the application.

Even if the default main thread creates the components before the EDT accesses them from the listener method, the EDT may have an inconsistent view (because of caching) and be unable to access the references to the new components. An application crash (probably a thrown java.lang.NullPointerException object) would most likely occur.

Listing B-1 presents the source code to ViewPage, a Swing application for viewing web page HTML. This application suffers from both problems.

Listing B-1. A Problematic Web Page HTML Viewer Swing Application

```java
import java.awt.BorderLayout;
import java.awt.Dimension;
import java.awt.EventQueue;

import java.awt.event.ActionEvent;
import java.awt.event.ActionListener;

import java.io.InputStream;
import java.io.IOException;

import java.net.URL;

import javax.swing.JFrame;
import javax.swing.JLabel;
import javax.swing.JPanel;
import javax.swing.JScrollPane;
import javax.swing.JTextArea;
import javax.swing.JTextField;

public class ViewPage
{
   public static void main(String[] args)
   {
      final JFrame frame = new JFrame("View Page");
      frame.setDefaultCloseOperation(JFrame.EXIT_ON_CLOSE);
      JPanel panel = new JPanel();
      panel.add(new JLabel("Enter URL"));
      final JTextField txtURL = new JTextField(40);
      panel.add(txtURL);
      frame.getContentPane().add(panel, BorderLayout.NORTH);
      final JTextArea txtHTML = new JTextArea(10, 40);
      frame.getContentPane().add(new JScrollPane (txtHTML),
                                 BorderLayout.CENTER);
      ActionListener al = (ae) ->
```

```
        {
            InputStream is = null;
            try
            {
                URL url = new URL(txtURL.getText());
                is = url.openStream();
                StringBuilder sb = new StringBuilder();
                int b;
                while ((b = is.read()) != -1)
                    sb.append((char) b);
                txtHTML.setText(sb.toString());
            }
            catch (IOException ioe)
            {
                txtHTML.setText(ioe.getMessage());
            }
            finally
            {
                txtHTML.setCaretPosition(0);
                if (is != null)
                    try
                    {
                        is.close();
                    }
                    catch (IOException ioe)
                    {
                    }
            }
        };
        txtURL.addActionListener(al);
        frame.pack();
        frame.setVisible(true);
    }
}
```

Listing B-1's main() method creates a GUI consisting of a text field for entering a web page's URL and a scrollable text area for displaying the page's HTML. Pressing the Enter key after entering the URL causes ViewPage to fetch and then display the HTML.

Compile Listing B-1 as follows:

```
javac ViewPage.java
```

Run the resulting application as follows:

```
java ViewPage
```

You should observe the GUI (populated with a sample URL and part of the resulting web page's HTML) shown in Figure B-1.

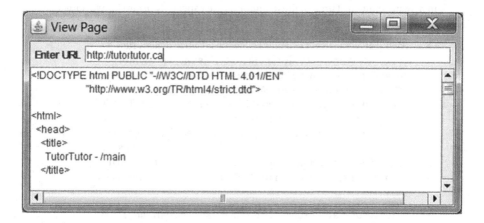

Figure B-1. *Entering a URL in a text field and viewing web page output in a scrollable text area*

The first problem with this application is that the GUI is created on the default main thread instead of on the EDT. Although you probably won't encounter a problem when you run ViewPage, there is potential for thread interference and memory inconsistency problems.

The second problem with this application is that the EDT, which runs the action listener in response to pressing Enter on the text field, is delayed by the code that opens an input stream to the URL and reads its content into a string builder. The GUI is unresponsive during this time.

Threading APIs

Swing provides APIs that overcome the aforementioned problems with the EDT. In this section, I introduce you to these APIs. I also introduce you to Swing's version of a timer, which is considerably different from the Timer Framework that I presented in Chapter 4.

SwingUtilities and EventQueue

The javax.swing.SwingUtilities class provides a collection of static methods that are useful in a Swing context. Three of these methods are especially useful for working with the EDT and avoiding the previous problems:

- void invokeAndWait(Runnable doRun): Cause doRun.run() to execute synchronously on the EDT. This call blocks until all pending events have been processed and (then) doRun.run() returns. invokeAndWait() throws java.lang. InterruptedException when this method is interrupted while waiting for the EDT to finish executing doRun.run(). It throws java.lang.reflect.InvocationTargetException when an exception is thrown from doRun.run(). invokeAndWait() should be used when an application thread needs to update the GUI from any thread other than the EDT. It shouldn't be called from the EDT.

- void invokeLater(Runnable doRun): Cause doRun.run() to be executed asynchronously on the EDT. This happens after all pending events have been processed. invokeLater() should be used when an application thread needs to update the GUI. It can be called from any thread.

- boolean isEventDispatchThread(): Return true when the invoking thread is the EDT; otherwise, return false.

The invokeAndWait(), invokeLater(), and isEventDispatchThread() methods are wrappers that call the equivalent methods in the java.awt.EventQueue class. Although you can prefix these methods with SwingUtilities, I use EventQueue as the prefix (out of habit).

You typically use invokeLater() to construct a Swing GUI according to the following pattern:

```
Runnable r = ... // ... refers to the runnable's anonymous class or lambda
EventQueue.invokeLater(r);
```

Listing B-2 presents the source code to a second version of ViewPage that uses invokeLater() to construct the Swing GUI on the EDT.

Listing B-2. Constructing the HTML Viewer Swing Application GUI on the EDT

```
import java.awt.BorderLayout;
import java.awt.Dimension;
import java.awt.EventQueue;

import java.awt.event.ActionEvent;
import java.awt.event.ActionListener;
```

```java
import java.io.InputStream;
import java.io.IOException;

import java.net.URL;

import javax.swing.JFrame;
import javax.swing.JLabel;
import javax.swing.JPanel;
import javax.swing.JScrollPane;
import javax.swing.JTextArea;
import javax.swing.JTextField;

public class ViewPage
{
    public static void main(String[] args)
    {
        Runnable r = () ->
        {
            final JFrame frame = new JFrame("View Page");
            frame.setDefaultCloseOperation(JFrame.EXIT_ON_CLOSE);
            JPanel panel = new JPanel();
            panel.add(new JLabel("Enter URL"));
            final JTextField txtURL = new JTextField(40);
            panel.add(txtURL);
            frame.getContentPane().add(panel, BorderLayout.NORTH);
            final JTextArea txtHTML = new JTextArea(10, 40);
            frame.getContentPane().add(new JScrollPane (txtHTML),
                                        BorderLayout.CENTER);
            ActionListener al = (ae) ->
            {
                InputStream is = null;
                try
                {
                    URL url = new URL(txtURL.getText());
                    is = url.openStream();
                    StringBuilder sb = new StringBuilder();
                    int b;
                    while ((b = is.read()) != -1)
                        sb.append((char) b);
                    txtHTML.setText(sb.toString());
                }
                catch (IOException ioe)
                {
                    txtHTML.setText(ioe.getMessage());
                }
```

```
            finally
            {
                txtHTML.setCaretPosition(0);
                if (is != null)
                    try
                    {
                        is.close();
                    }
                    catch (IOException ioe)
                    {
                    }
            }
        };
        txtURL.addActionListener(al);
        frame.pack();
        frame.setVisible(true);
    };
    EventQueue.invokeLater(r);
  }
}
```

Listing B-2 solves one problem but we still have to prevent the EDT from being delayed. We can solve this problem by creating a worker thread to read the page and use invokeAndWait() to update the scrollable text area with the page content on the EDT. Check out Listing B-3.

Listing B-3. Constructing the HTML Viewer Swing Application GUI on a Non-Delayed EDT

```
import java.awt.BorderLayout;
import java.awt.Dimension;
import java.awt.EventQueue;

import java.awt.event.ActionEvent;
import java.awt.event.ActionListener;

import java.io.InputStream;
import java.io.IOException;

import java.lang.reflect.InvocationTargetException;

import java.net.URL;

import javax.swing.JFrame;
import javax.swing.JLabel;
import javax.swing.JPanel;
import javax.swing.JScrollPane;
import javax.swing.JTextArea;
import javax.swing.JTextField;
```

```java
public class ViewPage
{
   public static void main(String[] args)
   {
      Runnable r = () ->
      {
         final JFrame frame = new JFrame("View Page");
         frame.setDefaultCloseOperation(JFrame.EXIT_ON_CLOSE);
         JPanel panel = new JPanel();
         panel.add(new JLabel("Enter URL"));
         final JTextField txtURL = new JTextField(40);
         panel.add(txtURL);
         frame.getContentPane().add(panel, BorderLayout.NORTH);
         final JTextArea txtHTML = new JTextArea(10, 40);
         frame.getContentPane().add(new JScrollPane (txtHTML),
                                    BorderLayout.CENTER);
         ActionListener al = (ae) ->
         {
            txtURL.setEnabled(false);
            Runnable worker = () ->
            {
               InputStream is = null;
               try
               {
                  URL url = new URL(txtURL.getText());
                  is = url.openStream();
                  final StringBuilder sb = new StringBuilder();
                  int b;
                  while ((b = is.read()) != -1)
                     sb.append((char) b);
                  Runnable r1 = () ->
                  {
                     txtHTML.setText(sb.toString());
                     txtURL.setEnabled(true);
                  };
                  try
                  {
                     EventQueue.invokeAndWait(r1);
                  }
                  catch (InterruptedException ie)
                  {
                  }
                  catch (InvocationTargetException ite)
                  {
                  }
               }
```

```
catch (final IOException ioe)
{
   Runnable r1 = () ->
   {
      txtHTML.setText(ioe.getMessage());
      txtURL.setEnabled(true);
   };
   try
   {
      EventQueue.invokeAndWait(r1);
   }
   catch (InterruptedException ie)
   {
   }
   catch (InvocationTargetException ite)
   {
   }
}
finally
{
   Runnable r1 = () ->
   {
      txtHTML.setCaretPosition(0);
      txtURL.setEnabled(true);
   };
   try
   {
      EventQueue.invokeAndWait(r1);
   }
   catch (InterruptedException ie)
   {
   }
   catch (InvocationTargetException ite)
   {
   }
   if (is != null)
      try
      {
         is.close();
      }
      catch (IOException ioe)
      {
      }
}
};
new Thread(worker).start();
};
txtURL.addActionListener(al);
```

```
        frame.pack();
        frame.setVisible(true);
    };
    EventQueue.invokeLater(r);
  }
}
```

I've chosen to disable the text field for further input when a page is being obtained and enable it afterward. You can still close the GUI at any time.

Although Listing B-3 solves the unresponsive GUI problem, the solution is somewhat verbose. Fortunately, there is an alternative solution.

SwingWorker

Swing provides the javax.swing.SwingWorker class to accommodate long-running tasks (such as reading URL content) with reduced verbosity. You must subclass this abstract class and override one or more methods to accomplish useful work.

SwingWorker's generic type is SwingWorker<T, V>. Parameters T and V identify the final and intermediate task result types, respectively.

You override the protected abstract T doInBackground() method to execute a long-running task on a worker thread and return a result of type T (Void is the return type when there is no result). When this method finishes, the protected void done() method is invoked on the EDT. By default, this method does nothing. However, you can override done() to safely update the GUI.

While the task is running, you can periodically publish results to the EDT by invoking the protected void publish(V... chunks) method. These results are retrieved by an overriding protected void process(List<V> chunks) method whose code runs on the EDT. If there are no intermediate results to process, you can specify Void for V (and avoid using the publish() and process() methods).

SwingWorker provides two more methods that you need to know about. First, void execute() schedules the invoking SwingWorker object for execution on a worker thread. Second, T get() waits if necessary for doInBackground() to complete and then returns the final result.

▪ **Note** SwingWorker's get() method throws an instance of the java.util.concurrent. ExecutionException class when an exception is thrown while attempting to retrieve the object returned from doInBackground(). It can also throw InterruptedException.

Listing B-4 presents the source code to a final ViewPage application that uses SwingWorker instead of invokeAndWait().

Listing B-4. Constructing the HTML Viewer Swing Application GUI on a Non-Delayed EDT, Revisited

```java
import java.awt.BorderLayout;
import java.awt.Dimension;
import java.awt.EventQueue;

import java.awt.event.ActionEvent;
import java.awt.event.ActionListener;

import java.io.InputStream;
import java.io.IOException;

import java.net.URL;

import java.util.concurrent.ExecutionException;

import javax.swing.JFrame;
import javax.swing.JLabel;
import javax.swing.JPanel;
import javax.swing.JScrollPane;
import javax.swing.JTextArea;
import javax.swing.JTextField;
import javax.swing.SwingWorker;

public class ViewPage
{
    public static void main(String[] args)
    {
        Runnable r = () ->
        {
            final JFrame frame = new JFrame("View Page");
            frame.setDefaultCloseOperation(JFrame.EXIT_ON_CLOSE);
            JPanel panel = new JPanel();
            panel.add(new JLabel("Enter URL"));
            final JTextField txtURL = new JTextField(40);
            panel.add(txtURL);
            frame.getContentPane().add(panel, BorderLayout.NORTH);
            final JTextArea txtHTML = new JTextArea(10, 40);
            frame.getContentPane().add(new JScrollPane (txtHTML),
                                    BorderLayout.CENTER);
            ActionListener al = (ae) ->
            {
                txtURL.setEnabled(false);
                class GetHTML extends SwingWorker<StringBuilder, Void>
```

```
{
    private final String url;

    GetHTML(String url)
    {
        this.url = url;
    }

    @Override
    public StringBuilder doInBackground()
    {
        StringBuilder sb = new StringBuilder();
        InputStream is = null;
        try
        {
            URL url = new URL(this.url);
            is = url.openStream();
            int b;
            while ((b = is.read()) != -1)
                sb.append((char) b);
            return sb;
        }
        catch (IOException ioe)
        {
            sb.setLength(0);
            sb.append(ioe.getMessage());
            return sb;
        }
        finally
        {
            if (is != null)
                try
                {
                    is.close();
                }
                catch (IOException ioe)
                {
                }
        }
    }
}
```

```
                @Override
                public void done()
                {
                    try
                    {
                        StringBuilder sb = get();
                        txtHTML.setText(sb.toString());
                        txtHTML.setCaretPosition(0);
                    }
                    catch (ExecutionException ee)
                    {
                        txtHTML.setText(ee.getMessage());
                    }
                    catch (InterruptedException ie)
                    {
                        txtHTML.setText("Interrupted");
                    }
                    txtURL.setEnabled(true);
                }
            }
            new GetHTML(txtURL.getText()).execute();
        };
        txtURL.addActionListener(al);
        frame.pack();
        frame.setVisible(true);
    };
    EventQueue.invokeLater(r);
  }
}
```

This final version of ViewPage relies on GetHTML, a local SwingWorker subclass that's declared in the action listener lambda body, to read the web page on a worker thread (keeping the user interface responsive), and update the user interface with the HTML on the EDT (where Swing code must execute).

When the lambda runs (the user presses Enter after entering a URL in the text field), it instantiates GetHTML with the text field's text (the text field isn't accessed from the worker thread because Swing is single-threaded) and calls SwingWorker's execute() method.

execute() causes GetHTML's overriding doInBackground() method to be called on a worker thread, which populates a java.lang.StringBuilder object with HTML/error text and returns this object. The EDT then calls the overriding done() method, which accesses the StringBuilder object by calling SwingWorker's get() method and populates the text area with these contents.

Timer

Swing provides the javax.swing.Timer class (as a simplified version of the Timer Framework—see Chapter 4) to periodically execute Swing code on the EDT. It fires an action event to registered listeners after an initial delay and repeatedly thereafter with events separated by between-event delays.

Call the Timer(int delay, ActionListener listener) constructor to create a timer with initial and between-event delays (in milliseconds), and with the initial action listener (which may be null) as the target of events that are sent every delay milliseconds.

The delay parameter value is used as both the initial delay and the between-event delay. You can also set these values separately by calling the void setInitialDelay(int initialDelay) and void setDelay(int delay) methods.

■ **Note** Invoke Timer's void setRepeats(boolean flag) method with a false argument to instruct the timer to send only a single action event.

Call void addActionListener(ActionListener listener) to add another action listener and void removeActionListener(ActionListener listener) to remove the previously registered action listener. Call ActionListener[] getActionListeners() to obtain all registered listeners.

The newly created timer is in its stopped state. To start the timer, call its void start() method. Conversely, you would call void stop() to terminate the timer. You might also want to call boolean isRunning() to determine if the timer is running.

Listing B-5 presents the source code to a Counter application that creates a timer to constantly display a running count via a label.

Listing B-5. Starting and Stopping a Count

```java
import java.awt.EventQueue;
import java.awt.FlowLayout;

import java.awt.event.ActionListener;

import javax.swing.JButton;
import javax.swing.JFrame;
import javax.swing.JLabel;
import javax.swing.JPanel;
import javax.swing.Timer;

public class Counter extends JFrame
{
    int count;
```

```java
    public Counter(String title)
    {
        super(title);
        setDefaultCloseOperation(EXIT_ON_CLOSE);

        JPanel pnl = new JPanel();
        ((FlowLayout) pnl.getLayout()).setHgap(20);
        final JLabel lblCount = new JLabel("");
        pnl.add(lblCount);
        final JButton btnStartStop = new JButton("Start");
        ActionListener al = (ae) ->
        {
            ++count;
            lblCount.setText(count + " ");
        };
        final Timer timer = new Timer(30, al);
        al = (ae) ->
        {
            if (btnStartStop.getText().equals("Start"))
            {
                btnStartStop.setText("Stop");
                timer.start();
            }
            else
            {
                btnStartStop.setText("Start");
                timer.stop();
            }
        };
        btnStartStop.addActionListener(al);
        pnl.add(btnStartStop);
        setContentPane(pnl);

        setSize(300, 80);
        setVisible(true);
    }

    public static void main(String[] args)
    {
        EventQueue.invokeLater(() -> new Counter("Counter"));
    }
}
```

Listing B-5's main() method creates a GUI consisting of a label and a Start/Stop button. The label displays the count variable's current value and the button text alternates between Start and Stop. Clicking the button when it indicates Start causes the timer to start; clicking the button when it indicates Stop causes the timer to stop. The timer action listener increments the count variable and displays its value via the label. The space character that's appended to count converts the expression to a string and ensures that its rightmost pixels are not cut off.

Compile Listing B-5 as follows:

```
javac Counter.java
```

Run the resulting application as follows:

```
java Counter
```

Figure B-2 shows the resulting GUI.

Figure B-2. *The panel's components are horizontally centered*

Timer-Based Slide Show

A *slide show* is a presentation of still images on a projection screen, typically in a prearranged sequence. Each image is usually displayed for at least a few seconds before being replaced by the next image.

A slide show involves a projector, a screen, and slides. The projector contains slides to be projected, the screen displays a projected slide image, and a slide contains an image and other attributes (such as a textual title).

I've created a Java application named SlideShow that lets you project arbitrary slideshows. Listing B-6 presents its source code.

Listing B-6. Describing a Timer-Based Slide Show

```
import java.awt.AlphaComposite;
import java.awt.Color;
import java.awt.Dimension;
import java.awt.EventQueue;
import java.awt.Font;
import java.awt.FontMetrics;
import java.awt.Graphics;
import java.awt.Graphics2D;
import java.awt.RenderingHints;
```

185

```java
import java.awt.event.ActionListener;
import java.awt.event.WindowAdapter;
import java.awt.event.WindowEvent;

import java.awt.image.BufferedImage;

import java.io.BufferedReader;
import java.io.File;
import java.io.FileReader;
import java.io.IOException;

import java.util.ArrayList;
import java.util.List;

import javax.imageio.ImageIO;

import javax.swing.JComponent;
import javax.swing.JFrame;
import javax.swing.Timer;

class Projector
{
    private volatile List<Slide> slides;
    private Screen s;
    private Timer t;
    private volatile int slideIndexC, slideIndexN;
    private volatile float weight;

    Projector(List<Slide> slides, Screen s)
    {
        this.slides = slides;
        this.s = s;
        t = new Timer(1500, null);
        t.setDelay(3000);
        slideIndexC = 0;
        slideIndexN = 1;
    }

    void start()
    {
        s.drawImage(Slide.blend(slides.get(0), null, 1.0f));
        ActionListener al = (ae) ->
        {
            weight = 1.0f;
            Timer t2 = new Timer(0, null);
            t2.setDelay(10);
            ActionListener al2 = (ae2) ->
```

```
        {
            Slide slideC = slides.get(slideIndexC);
            Slide slideN = slides.get(slideIndexN);
            BufferedImage bi = Slide.blend(slideC, slideN, weight);
            s.drawImage(bi);
            weight -= 0.01f;
            if (weight <= 0.0f)
            {
                t2.stop();
                slideIndexC = slideIndexN;
                slideIndexN = (slideIndexN + 1) % slides.size();
            }
        };
        t2.addActionListener(al2);
        t2.start();
    };
    t.addActionListener(al);
    t.start();
}

void stop()
{
    t.stop();
}
}

class Screen extends JComponent
{
    private Dimension d;
    private BufferedImage bi;
    private String text;

    Screen(int width, int height)
    {
        d = new Dimension(width, height);
    }

    void drawImage(BufferedImage bi)
    {
        this.bi = bi;
        repaint();
    }

    @Override
    public Dimension getPreferredSize()
    {
        return d;
    }
```

```java
    @Override
    public void paint(Graphics g)
    {
        int w = getWidth();
        int h = getHeight();
        g.drawImage(bi, Slide.WIDTH <= w ? (w - Slide.WIDTH) / 2 : 0,
                    Slide.HEIGHT <= h ? (h - Slide.HEIGHT) / 2 : 0, null);
    }
}

class Slide
{
    static int WIDTH, HEIGHT;

    private static int TEXTBOX_WIDTH, TEXTBOX_HEIGHT, TEXTBOX_X, TEXTBOX_Y;

    private BufferedImage bi;
    private String text;
    private static Font font;

    private Slide(BufferedImage bi, String text)
    {
        this.bi = bi;
        this.text = text;
        font = new Font("Arial", Font.BOLD, 20);
    }

    static BufferedImage blend(Slide slide1, Slide slide2, float weight)
    {
        BufferedImage bi1 = slide1.getBufferedImage();
        BufferedImage bi2 = (slide2 != null)
                          ? slide2.getBufferedImage()
                          : new BufferedImage(Slide.WIDTH, Slide.HEIGHT,
                                              BufferedImage.TYPE_INT_RGB);
        BufferedImage bi3 = new BufferedImage(Slide.WIDTH, Slide.HEIGHT,
                                              BufferedImage.TYPE_INT_RGB);
        Graphics2D g2d = bi3.createGraphics();
        g2d.setComposite(AlphaComposite.getInstance(AlphaComposite.SRC_OVER,
                                                    weight));
        g2d.drawImage(bi1, 0, 0, null);
        g2d.setComposite(AlphaComposite.getInstance(AlphaComposite.SRC_OVER,
                                                    1.0f - weight));
        g2d.drawImage(bi2, 0, 0, null);
        g2d.setColor(Color.BLACK);
        g2d.setRenderingHint(RenderingHints.KEY_ANTIALIASING,
                             RenderingHints.VALUE_ANTIALIAS_ON);
        g2d.setComposite(AlphaComposite.getInstance(AlphaComposite.SRC_OVER,
                                                    0.5f));
```

```
      g2d.fillRect(TEXTBOX_X, TEXTBOX_Y, TEXTBOX_WIDTH, TEXTBOX_HEIGHT);
      g2d.setComposite(AlphaComposite.getInstance(AlphaComposite.SRC_OVER,
                                              weight));
      g2d.setColor(Color.WHITE);
      g2d.setFont(font);
      FontMetrics fm = g2d.getFontMetrics();
      g2d.drawString(slide1.getText(), TEXTBOX_X + (TEXTBOX_WIDTH -
                    fm.stringWidth(slide1.getText())) / 2,
                    TEXTBOX_Y + TEXTBOX_HEIGHT / 2 + fm.getHeight() / 4);
      g2d.setComposite(AlphaComposite.getInstance(AlphaComposite.SRC_OVER,
                                              1.0f - weight));
      if (slide2 != null)
         g2d.drawString(slide2.getText(), TEXTBOX_X + (TEXTBOX_WIDTH -
                       fm.stringWidth(slide2.getText())) / 2, TEXTBOX_Y +
                       TEXTBOX_HEIGHT / 2 + fm.getHeight() / 4);
      g2d.dispose();
      return bi3;
   }

   BufferedImage getBufferedImage()
   {
      return bi;
   }

   String getText()
   {
      return text;
   }

   static List<Slide> loadSlides(String imagesPath) throws IOException
   {
      File imageFilesPath = new File(imagesPath);
      if (!imageFilesPath.isDirectory())
         throw new IOException(imagesPath + " identifies a file");
      List<Slide> slides = new ArrayList<>();
      try (FileReader fr = new FileReader(imagesPath + "/index");
           BufferedReader br = new BufferedReader(fr))
      {
         String line;
         while ((line = br.readLine()) != null)
         {
            String[] parts = line.split(",");
            File file = new File(imageFilesPath + "/" + parts[0] + ".jpg");
            System.out.println(file);
            BufferedImage bi = ImageIO.read(file);
            if (WIDTH == 0)
            {
               WIDTH = bi.getWidth();
```

```
                  HEIGHT = bi.getHeight();
                  TEXTBOX_WIDTH = WIDTH / 2 + 10;
                  TEXTBOX_HEIGHT = HEIGHT / 10;
                  TEXTBOX_Y = HEIGHT - TEXTBOX_HEIGHT - 5;
                  TEXTBOX_X = (WIDTH - TEXTBOX_WIDTH) / 2;
               }
            slides.add(new Slide(bi, parts[1]));
         }
      }
      if (slides.size() < 2)
         throw new IOException("at least one image must be loaded");
      return slides;
   }
}

public class SlideShow
{
   public static void main(String[] args) throws IOException
   {
      if (args.length != 1)
      {
         System.err.println("usage: java SlideShow ssdir");
         return;
      }
      List<Slide> slides = Slide.loadSlides(args[0]);
      final Screen screen = new Screen(Slide.WIDTH, Slide.HEIGHT);
      final Projector p = new Projector(slides, screen);
      Runnable r = () ->
      {
         final JFrame f = new JFrame("Slide Show");
         WindowAdapter wa = new WindowAdapter()
                           {
                              @Override
                              public void windowClosing(WindowEvent we)
                              {
                                 p.stop();
                                 f.dispose();
                              }
                           };
         f.addWindowListener(wa);
         f.setContentPane(screen);
         f.pack();
         f.setVisible(true);
         p.start();
      };
      EventQueue.invokeLater(r);
   }
}
```

Listing B-6 models a slide show in terms of Projector, Screen, Slide, and SlideShow classes. Projector declares several private fields, a Projector(List<Slide> slides, Screen s) constructor for initializing a projector to a java.util.List of Slide objects and a Screen object, a void start() method for starting the projector, and a void stop() method for stopping the projector.

Screen, which subclasses javax.swing.JComponent to make a Screen instance a special kind of Swing component, declares several private fields, a Screen(int width, int height) constructor for instantiating this component to the extents of the screen passed to width and height, and a void drawImage(BufferedImage bi) method for drawing the buffered image passed to this method on the screen's surface. This class also overrides Dimension getPreferredSize() and void paint(Graphics g) to return the component's preferred size and to paint its surface.

Slide declares various constants, several private fields, a private Slide(BufferedImage bi, String text) constructor for initializing a Slide object, BufferedImage getBufferedImage() and String getText() getter methods for returning the slide's buffered image and text, a BufferedImage blend(Slide slide1, Slide slide2, float weight) class method for blending a pair of buffered images to show a transition between slides, and a List<Slide> loadSlides(String imagesPath) class method to load all slide images.

The blend() method extracts the buffered images associated with its slide arguments and blends these images together with the amount of blending determined by weight's value (which must lie in the range 0.0 through 1.0). The higher the value passed to weight, the more of slide1's image that contributes to the returned buffered image. After blending the images, blend() blends a pair of text strings over the blended image. The java.awt.AlphaComposite class is used to take care of blending in each case.

I've designed blend() to handle a special case where null is passed to slide2. This happens at the beginning of Projector's start() method where it executes s.drawImage(Slide.blend(slides.get(0), null, 1.0f)); to display the first slide—there's no transition at this point.

The loadSlides() method looks for a text file named index in the directory identified by this method's string argument and creates the List of Slides in the order identified by this text file's contents—you can choose an order to display slides that differs from the order of the image files stored in the directory. Each line is organized as a file name followed by a comma, which is followed by a textual description (such as **earth, Terran System**). When specifying a file name, you don't specify a file extension; loadSlides() is hardwired to recognize JPEG files only.

SlideShow declares a main() method that drives this application. This method first verifies that a single command-line argument identifying the slide show directory (a directory containing index and the JPEG files) has been specified. It then invokes loadSlides() to load index and all slide images from this directory. loadSlides() throws java.io.IOException when it's unable to load an image or when the number of images is less than 2. After all, how can you have a slide show with less than two images?

main() next creates a Screen component object for displaying slide images. It passes the width and height of each slide (actually, the width and height of each slide image) to Screen's constructor, which ensures that the screen is just large enough to display these slides. (All slide images must have the same width and height, although I don't enforce this requirement in loadSlides().)

The only remaining significant model object to create is the projector, and main() accomplishes this task by passing the List of Slide objects returned from loadSlides() and the previously created Screen object to Projector's constructor.

main()'s final task is to cause the GUI to be constructed on the EDT. This thread sets the content pane to the Screen object and invokes Projector's void start() method to begin the slide show. It also creates a window listener that invokes Projector's void stop() method when the user attempts to close the window. The window is then disposed.

Projector uses a pair of Timer objects to manage the slide show. The main timer object is responsible for advancing the projector to the next slide, and the subordinate timer object (which is created each time the main timer fires an action event) is responsible for transitioning from the currently displayed slide image to the next slide's image (with help from blend()).

Each timer instance runs on the EDT. It's important that the main timer not execute a timer task while the subordinate timer is running. If this rule isn't followed, the slide show will malfunction. I've chosen a period of 3000 milliseconds between successive executions of the main timer task and 10 milliseconds between successive executions of the subordinate timer task, which runs 100 times for an approximate total of 1000 milliseconds. When the subordinate timer task finishes, it stops itself.

Compile Listing B-6 as follows:

```
javac SlideShow.java
```

Assuming a Windows operating system, run the resulting application as follows:

```
java SlideShow ..\ss
```

ss identifies the example solar system slide show (included in this book's code) and is located in the parent directory of the current directory.

Figure B-3 shows the resulting GUI.

Figure B-3. *SlideShow horizontally centers a slide's text near the bottom of the slide*

Index

■ T, U

■ V

■ W, X, Y, Z

Get the eBook for only $5!

Why limit yourself?

Now you can take the weightless companion with you wherever you go and access your content on your PC, phone, tablet, or reader.

Since you've purchased this print book, we're happy to offer you the eBook in all 3 formats for just $5.

Convenient and fully searchable, the PDF version enables you to easily find and copy code—or perform examples by quickly toggling between instructions and applications. The MOBI format is ideal for your Kindle, while the ePUB can be utilized on a variety of mobile devices.

To learn more, go to www.apress.com/companion or contact support@apress.com.

Printed in the United States
By Bookmasters